Stress Management:
An Integrated Approach

Stress Management: An Integrated Approach

Dr Viswanathan Gopalan

GenNext Publication

ISBN: 978-93-5324-104-9

Price : ₹ 490/-

First Published, 2016

Published by

GenNext Publication
5, Ansari Road
Daryaganj, New Delhi-110002
Phone: 9811692060
E-mail: gennextpublication@hotmail.com

Printed at: G. Print Process, Delhi.

Cataloging in Publication Data—DK
Courtesy: D.K. Agencies (P) Ltd. <docinfo@dkagencies.com>

Gopalan, Viswanathan, author.
Stress management : an integrated approach / Viswanathan Gopalan.
pages cm
Includes bibliographical references.
ISBN: 978-93-5324-104-9

1. Stress management. I. Title.

RA785.G67 2016 DDC 155.9042 23

Contents

Acknowledgements

I acknowledge and thank all my friends, fellow professionals and researchers, who sincerely wished that I should publish one book on Stress Management after my second on Knowledge Management in 2015. Their constant support has been definitely motivating.

Special thanks and appreciation to my loved ones and family members including my dear wife Indira, daughter Sharmila, her husband Arjun and my son Vivek who constantly lent me encouragement and words of appreciation to keep me inspired to complete my mission.

It will not be appropriate if I do not acknowledge the initiative shown and the support given by Shri B P Garg and Shri Amit Garg, Directors, Gyan Books Pvt Ltd, in ensuring publication of this book. I wish to thank all members of their team from production, publication and marketing, who lent active support to make this happen.

I wish to congratulate and thank all the readers who read, enjoy and stand to benefit from this book which is intended to enhance their awareness and skills to manage stress in an integrated manner, which is a very critical challenge in today's fast paced and complex life.

I thank God for giving me this opportunity to serve Humanity by sharing the knowledge I have managed to acquire on this subject,with His Blessings and Grace.

1-6-2016 **Dr Viswanathan Gopalan**
Pune, India

Foreword

Living in the Twenty-first Century, in a modern world, a man's lifestyle is propelled by such factors as fast-track, fast food and a fast life. Further, the more one is ambitious, his much-compelling circumstances result in a spin-off that is the stressful period. Life is like music: if it loses it rhythm, it would be a disaster. The ancient Indian culture and its valued precepts of yoga have underscored the need for coordination between the body and mind so that the synergy can enable one to achieve equilibrium and equanimity in his attitude and functionality. Richard Carlson, the author of, "Don't Sweat the small stuff and it's all small stuff," calls upon everyone to set aside a quiet time for every day: "Whether it's ten minutes of meditation or yoga, or spending a little time in nature, or locking the bathroom and taking a ten-minute, quiet time is a vital part of life. Like spending time alone, it helps to balance the noise and confusion that infiltrate much of our day." In short, you don't have to worry if you are not in a hurry. The book of Dr Viswanathan Gopalan, "Stress Management – An Integrated Approach", clearly guides us as to how we should handle stress and go forward in our lives where mundane things overtake the essential ones and make us drift away from things of higher order.

Stress is an issue affecting all of us in the modern era of speed, competition and pressure to achieve. This book aims at bringing to the doorsteps of the reader, all the knowledge and skills he requires to identify, understand, manage and win over stress. A number of books have already been written on stress management. This book is unique in the sense that it covers all the techniques and skills known for identifying and managing stress in an integrated manner, including approaches such as positive thinking, exercises, relaxation, laughter, playing with children, travel, yoga, meditation and prayer, making the knowledge complete and usable by everyone. He has discussed with great knowledge, awareness and understanding, a step-by-step pathway as to how stress can be managed, sometimes combated and won over to enable people to lead a fully integrated existence with peace, happiness and health.

A senior colleague of mine had, on an occasion, was a victim of electrical shock due to electricity leakage and when the doctor did not find his blood pressure to be high as a result of this phenomenon, the officer wittily expressed that he had normally passed on the pressure to his staff and he, in turn, was not under pressure. Jokes apart, the ability not to get agitated or annoyed and as a result avoiding stress is dependent on one's capacity to maintain his equilibrium.

Planned day-to-day work will only enhance the efficiency and effectiveness of an individual apart from reducing the possible stress when the life is chaotic or disorderly. No doubt, the eustress and distress are the two aspects of stress as in the case of good cholesterol and bad cholesterol. There are people who, at times, are quite motivated to pursue their target or objectives and the eustress can make them do things better driven by the force of achievement. However, in the case of those who fail to achieve, the element of distress would land them in depression as well.

Dr Viswanathan Gopalan has been an engineer, a corporate manager, a professor in management, a trainer and a researcher. He has also been a social worker, key member of Vidya Vrikshah, an NGO dedicated to helping the Visually Challenged Children, headquartered in Chennai. He has authored already written and published two books titled, *'Motivation-The Essence of Living'* and *'Knowledge Management – In Organisations and in Personal Lives'*.

This book on Stress Management can be read and appreciated by all in the academic and research communities, organisations in the public and private domains, and the common man. The knowledge that Dr Viswanathan has shared in this book with the reader is useful and inspiring. I would recommend that those who are caught between the target deadlines and pressure of work study this book to bring back the rhythm in their personal lives by sharing their precious time for both the family and the employer organisation in a purposeful manner.

Chennai
June 21, 2016

K.V.S. Gopalakrishnan
Formerly Spl. Director,
Intelligence Bureau

Chapter - 1

Introduction to Stress Management

"If you want to conquer the anxiety of life, live in the moment, live in the breath." *Amit Ray, Om Chanting and Meditation*

Although the phenomenon of stress has existed since ancient times, attempts to study stress scientifically and systematically have been made only since the later half of the twentieth century. During the seventeenth century, human beings understood stress as something that caused hardship and caused affliction to them. In the eighteenth and nineteenth centuries the concept of force, pressure and strain related to stress was introduced (Ref 3, 4).

Social sciences and engineering during this period introduced the concepts of load as external to any solid body and the reaction from within the solid body as stress. The changes including the dimensional elongation were termed strain. Social and biological sciences discovered that all these concepts which applied to physical objects can be extended to the biology and psychology of the human beings too.

The impact and effects of stress on human health was analysed and systematically studied in the twentieth century by the 'Father of Stress Management', Dr Hans Selye (Ref 5). In the year 1951, he wrote his first article on stress and ever since, millions of research papers and articles on stress have appeared in journals and magazines on stress for the information, knowledge and understanding of all of us.

The purpose of this book is to bring all the available knowledge on stress to the reader under one banner called 'Stress Management-

An integrated approach', entirely for his benefit and all those who surround him and interact with him to share knowledge.

The Effect of Stress on Society

Stress is very expensive. Let's look at the statistics:

- Stress is recognised as the number one killer today. The American Medical Association stated that stress is the cause of 80 to 85 per cent of all human illness and disease or at the very least has a detrimental effect on our health and welfare of human beings.
- Every week, millions of people across the globe suffer some kind of stress related symptoms for which they need to take medication.
- Businesses in the world lose billions of dollars per year to stress related productivity loss and other cost. To put this in perspective, this amount is higher than the total cost related to all strikes and the net profit from all leading multinational companies.
- A famous research institute on stress estimates that 90 per cent of all visits to doctors are for stress-related disorders. In women, stress has been linked to fatigue, hair loss, bad complexion, insomnia, disruption of the menstrual cycle, low libido and lack of orgasm, among others. There is even evidence that it can increase your risk of more serious problems such as high blood pressure and heart disease.
- Stress speeds up your entire system and produces conditions in younger people that are more commonly associated with growing old. Virtually no part of your body can escape the ravages of stress.
- Studies show that stress can reduce the power of our immune systems. A study in the U.K. exposed 266 people to a common cold virus and then tracked who became sick. 28.6 per cent of those with few signs of stress caught the cold. However, the figure jumped to 42.4 per cent for those who were under high stress.
- Other studies show that women who have trouble coping with stress may be at risk of building up dangerous abdominal

fat. A study at a famous University on obese women shows that those with abdominal fat (apple shaped) secreted more stress hormones than those who carry extra weight on their hips (pear shaped). It is known that apple-shaped people are more at risk of heart disease.

- Stress increases heart rate and blood pressure. It changes the inner lining of our blood vessels, making our blood more likely to clot. Stress may change the way cholesterol is handled by our blood vessels and, in doing so, may increase plaque formation.

How Stress Gets Generated

Stress can often generated from sources we hardly ever imagine. An example will help you understand how this happens in your normal life.

Imagine that you have earned your first vacation out of your newly taken, highly paid job in an international firm of repute. You are a young guy living in one of the fast growing cities in India, the hub for industries and business. You have a lovely apartment in a posh locality and just bought a nice car. Your company has provided you with a driver who is taking you in your new car, to the airport to catch a flight in the afternoon and you have one hour to reach the airport. You are dreaming how you are going to enjoy the holiday in the sea resort where you have booked your accommodation in a posh hotel for the next week or so.

All on a sudden, the car comes to a screeching halt. You wake up from your dream and find that there is a huge procession of cars, may be a mile long in front of you. You are told by the driver that it will take an hour for the traffic to clear. You look back trough the rear window. The situation is bad. There is a long row of cars blocking your way to reverse. You understand that you stand to miss the flight and ruin the plan you had for reaching the destination you that day.

Your heart pounds fast and you sweat slightly. You start verbally abusing the crowd, the traffic, the drivers including yours and the government of the state for no fault of theirs.

You are in STRESS!

Your mind or brain immediately takes over. The middle and lower part of your brain electrically triggers a massive fight or flight response. Your body dumps sugars and fats into your bloodstream for quick energy and strength. Other chemicals released by the brain prepare your blood to clot more quickly, to reduce the possible blood loss in case of an anticipated accident. You feel your heart pounding in your chest and temples. Your brain is receiving more oxygen to sharpen your senses and coordination.

What you had just undergone is how stress works and how we cope with it. This is an example of a stress that was triggered by events or stimuli from outside your body. Other examples of stress that results from outside events are job-related stress (such as when your boss gives you unreasonable jobs, working with unreasonable customers), relationship induced stress (such as marital problems, death of a spouse, divorce), money problems (such as when all bills come due in January and you don't have money to pay for it), etc.

In the example cited above, when you think of the possibility of missing the flight, you get stressed. Some people get a stress attack when they just think of the possibility of getting involved in an accident while they drive on the road. This type of stress is called mind stressor. The origin of the stress, in this case, is within you.

Let us say that you actually miss the flight that day. However, you manage to go home and organise the same flight the next day at the same time. You are so upset you cannot sleep that night. Your muscles are very tense. Now you start worrying about your inability to sleep or about your body aches and pains. This creates more stress. See how this is triggering a domino effect.

Stress can also originate from emotional and psychological causes. For example, thinking of an accident or a pending annual appraisal for performance can make people anxious, may make it difficult for people to sleep. Then they worry about not getting enough sleep and how they will go to work without sleep. And so on. One stressful event leads to another and, if we don't control it, the domino effect kicks in, resulting in more accumulated stress which needs a release for the wellbeing and health of the person.

Even joyous events, such as getting married, a job promotion, buying a new home, or the birth of a child, can cause a great amount of stress. You also might get stressed out if you cannot achieve a particular goal or satisfy a certain wish. For instance, you may want very much to have a child but you and your wife cannot conceive. Fertility tests can't explain any reasons for this, and you feel very frustrated. You wonder why this situation happening to you. You even start blaming God for making you go through this difficulty. Certainly this is a very emotional issue- and one that you do not have much control over- A situation like this can generate enormous stress in your life. You may not have the skills to cope. You can go in to depression or worse.

Stress also exists in tandem with the pressure you feel when you perceive that negative consequences are attached to your actions. For instance, you might feel pressured to maintain a certain level of performance at work or else risk getting fired. If you find yourself thinking in this way, you should stop and consider whether the threat is real or if you are just being too hard on yourself. You might be able to control and even eliminate this kind of stress from your life.

Stress also stems from conflict, which is not always negative. For instance, a conflict could occur in having to choose between two positive goals of equal value, such as choosing between two excellent job offers. Or your conflict could involve a choice that has both a positive and negative outcome, such as you're getting married but it necessitates your moving across the country away from family and friends.

The Purpose of this Book

The author aims to share with you through this book, all important information and useful knowledge on stress and its effective management for your welfare. The book deals with, in an exhaustive way, fundamentals like what is stress, its definition, symptoms of understanding stress and its awareness, positive and negative stresses, ways of coping with stress, higher level ways to address stress, like yoga, meditation and prayer. In short, the book aims to tell you how you can integrate all these multifarious means of managing stress in a comprehensive, coordinated, integrated manner, so as to gain maximum benefit with regard to health and turn happiness. Please read on and enjoy the journey.

Chapter - 2

Definition, Nature and Mechanism of Stress

"A positive attitude may not solve all our problems but that is the only option we have if we want to get out of problems."
–*Subodh Gupta, Stress Management a Holistic Approach*

What is Stress? (Ref 2, 3, 4)

When demands are placed on an individual in a work situation or in personal life, he or she experiences stress. This is, many times, unavoidable in life. In fact, without these kinds of stress, life can become boring and dull. This will be a positive way to look at the presence of stress in our lives.

A certain amount of stress is even desirable to make us enjoy the work we do. However, the problem arises, when the stress we face exceeds certain limits making it difficult to manage. If high levels of stress is prolonged, the individual faces fatigue and exhaustion both mentally and physically. This can be called negative stress or distress. Distress accumulated for long periods of time leads to disorders, mental and physical in the individual, leading to diseases and sometimes even death.

Distress affects our health, vitality, increases our vulnerability and leads to a life style that is dysfunctional and unfulfilled. The person may become neurotic or even psychotic while living a sad, unhappy life. He can become a burden to himself and society. Tendencies to end one's own life are very common among these types of individuals.

In the following chapters of this book, we will be looking at these aspects in great detail. In this chapter, we are going to discuss some of the more fundamental issues related to the definition, nature and mechanisms of stress.

Definition of Stress

Dictionary defines stress as pressure, a condition causing disquiet. Let us look at the definitions given by authorities on stress. We will consider a couple of them.

Definition 1

'Stress is the non-specific response of the body to any demands made upon it'–Dr Hans Selye (Ref 5)

Definition 2

'An adaptive response to an external situation that results in physical, psychological and/or behavioural deviations for organisational participants' – Fred Luthens

The second definition by Fred Luthens is spelled in an organisational context. However, the definitions talk about the relevance of stress with regard to human conditions and hence, significantly applicable to all human beings.

Nature of Stress

It is clear from the above definitions; stress is induced by external demands made on the human being, but is related and decided by his ability to cope with it psychologically, emotionally and behaviourally. A combination of all the reactions of the human to an external stressor or an event causing stress from a behavioural and psychological point of view eventually decides how the stress is going to affect the individual.

Several factors play a role in deciding the psychological and behavioural responses of an individual to a given situation which can be termed stressful. They are:

1. Family and parental background
2. Education
3. Influence of parents
4. Influence of teachers

5. Influence of friends
6. Influence of neighbours
7. Experiences of the past
8. Present circumstances and experiences
9. Expectations about future
10. Attitudes of the individual
11. Belief systems
12. Age and maturity level
13. Physical fitness level of the individual
14. Life style and habits

And so on.

In a general manner, we can say that stress is decided by four factors acting in combination which decides its magnitude and impact. They are:

1. The external demands
2. The internal needs of an individual
3. The coping resources- internal to an individual
4. The coping resources- external available to the individual

Models of Stress- by Researchers and Experts

There are generalised models on stress which have evolved historically since the start of the twentieth century. They are:

- The "emergency response" / fight-or-flight response by Walter Cannon (1914, 1932),
- "General Adaptation Syndrome" by Hans Selye (1936),
- "Transactional (or cognitive) Stress Model" / stress model of Lazarus after Lazarus (1974),
- "Theory of resource conservation" by Stevan Hobfoll (1988, 1998; Hobfoll and Buchwald, 2004).

Transactional Model

Richard Lazarus and Susan Folkman (Ref 6) suggested in 1984 that stress can be thought of as resulting from an "imbalance between demands and resources" or as occurring when "pressure exceeds one's perceived ability to cope". Stress management was developed and premised on the idea that stress is not a direct response to a stressor but rather one's resources and ability to cope mediate the stress response and are amenable to change, thus allowing stress to be controllable.

According to the research by Lazarus and Folkman, among the many stressors mentioned by employees of an organisation, these are the most common:

- The way employees are treated by their bosses/supervisors or company
- Lack of job security
- Company policies
- Coworkers who don't do their fair share
- Unclear expectations
- Poor communication
- Not enough control over assignments
- Inadequate pay or benefits
- Urgent deadlines
- Too much work
- Long hours
- Uncomfortable physical conditions
- Relationship conflicts
- Coworkers making careless mistakes
- Dealing with rude customers
- Lack of cooperation
- How the company treats coworkers

In order to develop an effective stress management programme it is first necessary to identify the factors that are central to a person controlling his/her stress, and to identify the intervention methods which effectively target these factors. Lazarus and Folkman's interpretation of stress focuses on the transaction between people and their external environment (known as the Transactional Model). The model contends that stress may not be a stressor if the person does not perceive the stressor as a threat but rather as positive or even challenging. Also, if the person possesses or can use adequate coping skills, then stress may not actually be a result or develop because of the stressor. The model proposes that people can be taught to manage their stress and cope with their stressors. They may learn to change their perspective of the stressor and provide them with the ability and confidence to improve their lives and handle all types of stressors.

Health Realisation/Innate Health Model

The health realisation/innate health model of stress is also founded on the idea that stress does not necessarily follow the presence of a potential stressor. Instead of focusing on the individual's appraisal of so-called stressors in relation to his or her own coping skills (as the transactional model does), the health realisation model focuses on the nature of thought, stating that it is ultimately a person's thought processes that determine the response to potentially stressful external circumstances. In this model, stress results from appraising oneself and one's circumstances through a mental filter of insecurity and negativity, whereas a feeling of wellbeing results from approaching the world with a "quiet mind".

This model proposes that helping stressed individuals understand the nature of thought—especially providing them with the ability to recognise when they are in the grip of insecure thinking, disengage from it, and access natural positive feelings—will reduce their stress.

The Mechanism of Stress-Our Body's Reaction to Stress (General Adaptation Syndrome (GAS) by Dr Hans Selye-1936 (Ref 5)

Dr Hans Selye, as we mentioned earlier, is considered the 'Father of Stress Management'. He has contended that when stress is encountered by a human being, the body and mind respond by an adaptation process known as the General Adaptation Syndrome or shortly called GAS.

When a person experiences stress, the brain responds by initiating 1400 different responses including the dumping of a variety of chemicals to our blood stream. This gives a momentary boost to do whatever needs to be done to survive. If left unchecked, however, the person can have a heart attack or stroke. Many people start drinking alcohol. They get depressed, find it difficult to sleep, experience chest pain. The body runs out of the immunity to fight diseases. So, very often, these persons die of disease such as cancer, pneumonia, etc. The stress will never be identified as the cause of the death. I call the stress the proxy killer. Some other disease always takes the blame for it.

Doctors call the body's reaction to stress as General Adaptation Syndrome (GAS). There are three stages to GAS.

In the first stage of GAS called alarm reaction, the body releases adrenaline and a variety of other psychological mechanisms to combat the stress and to stay in control. This is called fight or flight response. The muscles tense, the heart beats faster, the breathing and perspiration increases, the eyes dilate, the stomach may clench. Believe it or not, this is done by nature to protect you in case something bad happens. Once the cause of the stress is removed, the body will go back to normal.

If the cause for the stress is not removed, GAS goes to its second stage called resistance or adaptation. This is the body's response to long-term protection. It secretes further hormones that increase blood sugar levels to sustain energy and raise blood pressure. The adrenal cortex (outer covering) produces hormones called corticosteroids for this resistance reaction. Overuse by the body's defence mechanism in this phase eventually leads to disease. If this adaptation phase continues for a prolonged period of time without periods of relaxation and rest to counterbalance the stress response, sufferers become prone to fatigue, concentration lapses, irritability and lethargy as the effort to sustain arousal slides into negative stress.

The third stage of GAS is called exhaustion. In this stage, the body has run out of its reserve of body energy and immunity. Mental, physical and emotional resources suffer heavily. The body experiences "adrenal exhaustion". The blood sugar levels decrease as the adrenals become depleted, leading to decreased stress tolerance, progressive mental and physical exhaustion, illness and collapse.

The hypothalamus-pituitary-adrenal (HPA) chain of command has served humans well as a means of survival for thousands of years. However, for those suffering from chronic anxiety and depression this process malfunctions. Continual stress early in life disrupts the cycle. Instead of shutting off once the crisis is over, the process continues, with the hypothalamus continuing to signal the adrenals to produce cortisol. This increased cortisol production exhausts the stress mechanism, leading to fatigue and depression. Cortisol also interferes with serotonin activity, furthering the depressive effect.

Continually high cortisol levels lead to suppression of the immune system through increased production of interleukin-6, an immune-system messenger. This coincides with research findings indicating that stress and depression have a negative effect on the immune system. Reduced immunity makes the body more susceptible to everything from cold and flu to cancer. For example, the incidence of serious illness, including cancer, is significantly higher among people who have suffered the death of a spouse in the previous year. Fortunately, this immune-suppression process can be corrected with psychotherapy, medication, or any number of other positive influences that restore hope and a feeling of self-esteem. The ability of human beings to recover from adversity is remarkable.

Thus, very often, those under severe, prolonged stress may contract diseases related to immune deficiency and may even die of these diseases. The death does not come from stress itself. What happens is that the body loses all its resistance in its effort to ward off the stress. Thus, the persons die of immune deficiency causes such as infection, cancer etc. So, it is very important that we recognise the cause for stresses and remove the causes to maintain a healthy lifestyle.

Another result of stress is the clogging of the arteries by the fat and cholesterol released by the body during the attempt to fight stress. This may result in a heart attack or you may suffer a stroke by losing blood supply to the brain. Many people start drinking to combat the stress. Stress can also manifest itself into a number of diseases – depression, headaches, insomnia, ulcers, asthma, and more.

Major Stressors in Life – List by Thomas Homes and Richard Rahe

Numerous life events-such as: the death of a family member or friend, the loss of a job, buying a house or moving, and having a child, cause stress. Thomas Holmes and Richard Rahe, developed a list of major life stressors. These are listed in descending order below, beginning with the most stressful event:

- Death of a spouse

- Divorce
- Marital separation
- Imprisonment
- Death of a close relative
- Personal injury or illness
- Marriage
- Fired from a job
- Marital reconciliation
- Retirement
- Illness of a relative
- Pregnancy
- Sexual problems
- Birth or adoption
- Business readjustment
- Change in financial status
- Death of a close friend
- Change to different work
- Increased arguments with spouse
- Mortgage or loan for major purchase
- Foreclosure on mortgage or loan
- Change in job responsibilities
- Child leaving home
- Problems with in-laws
- Outstanding personal achievement
- Spouse begins or stops work
- Begin or end school
- Change in living conditions
- Changing personal habits
- Problems with your boss
- Change in work hours/conditions
- Change in residence or school
- Recreation
- Church or social activities

- Mortgage or loan for smaller purchase
- Change in sleeping habits
- Change in family gatherings
- Change in eating habits
- Vacation
- Christmas
- Minor law violations

It is interesting to note that Homes and Rahe have placed the death of a spouse at the top of the scale, while a severe stressor such as imprisonment has been kept three levels below. Happy occasions like a marriage or a vacation or Christmas can be stressful depending on the levels of urgency, volume of work and responsibilities involved and the psychological, physical and other resources the persons concerned have to muster in order to make these events happen.

In the next chapter we are going to learn about the symptoms of the body and mind which individuals can recognise in order to understand that they are stress afflicted and hence need to intervene and take remedial measures to cope and combat if necessary.

Chapter - 3

Classification, Sources, Personality Types and Stress

"Laughter is the only medicine, without side effects."

–Shannon L. Alder

Classification (Ref 2, 3, 4)

Stress can be classified according to different criteria. Some are mentioned below:

1. **According to Effect**
   - *Eustress or positive stress:* When a person experiences a sense of elation while doing an activity, let us say, like going on a tour of a foreign country for the first time and enjoying the visit is an example.
   - *Disstress or negative stress:* Unable to answer questions in an examination because the individual finds them tough and the time constraint is severe is one example that makes it clear.
   - *Neustress or indifference to stress:* Sitting in front of TV and watching a dull programme without enjoying it just in order to kill time will be a good example to indicate this situation which is stressful.
2. **According to Avoidability**
   - *Avoidable stress:* e.g., Expecting too much out of a relationship with a friend.
   - *Non-avoidable stress:* e.g., Death of some one very old known to you for a long time.

3. **According to Intensity**
   - *Life threatening:* e.g., Getting hurt in an accident.
   - *Non-life threatening:* e.g., Facing an impending examination
4. **According to Levels**
   - *Extrinsic Stress:* At an Organisational Level
   - *Intrinsic Stress:* At an Individual Level
5. **According to Source of Stress**

   Examples
   - Adjustment Stress
   - Adaptability Stress
   - Confusion Stress
   - Conviction Stress
   - Ego Stress
   - Situational Stress
   - Frustration Stress

Sources of Stress – Stressors

The root causes or sources of stress are called stressors. Stressors precipitate and cause stress to happen in an individual. They can be classified, broadly, in to three types, which are:

1. Physical Stressors
2. Social Stressors
3. Psychological Stressors

Physical Stressors: These are factors outside the individual physically away from him such as pollutants, chemicals, drugs, poisonous environment, radiation, excessive climates such as extreme heat, extreme cold, humidity, noise, vibration etc. These physical stressors are all around us without sometimes our being unaware of their presence. Constant exposure to physical stressors can be highly damaging to health both physical as well as mental in the long run.

Social Stressors: These are also external to an individual. However, the difference between social stressors and physical stressors is that, social stressors result from interactions between and among individuals. Examples are, events such as attending parties, giving speeches, expressing anger, disharmony in relationships such as between a father and an adult son, death of a family member and so on.

Many of the social stressors are 'unavoidable' like the death of a close relative, loss of a job, changing the residence and moving in to a new residential locality where strangers are encountered and one needs to build new social relationships. These are recurrent in life. One needs to adjust and cope with social stressors fast. Else, it takes its toll on the individual in the form of illnesses, physical, mental and emotional.

Psychological Stressors: These types of stressors can be the most debilitating or damaging for health. Psychological stressors stem from physical as well as social stressors. In addition, they are also 'self-induced'. By self-induced, we mean the individual brings about stress on himself through negative thoughts, negative perceptions and negative emotions. Some examples of psychological stressors are emotions and feelings like anger, guilt, worry, resentment, self-pity, hatred and so on.

Negative 'self-talk' about oneself such as calling oneself 'stupid', 'worthless' or 'I am a loser', 'I can never win' etc., are very strong labels of psychological stressors. A lot of attention and awareness on these kinds of self-induced stressors are necessary in order that the individual can identify and get rid of them eventually for greater health, happiness, peace and welfare.

Personality Types and Stress

A lot of research has been done to link and connect traits of individuals with different personality traits and the effect of stress on them. Traits such as dominance, aggressiveness, authoritarianism, tolerance to ambiguity, need for achievement, ability to handle anxiety etc., have been taken into consideration while carrying out this research. We will discuss in this section some of those correlations which are relevant to stress management.

Personalities of individuals have been classified into certain definite categories depending upon the thoughts, emotions, behaviour and attitude one displays under life situations. It is believed and research has proven that people who fall into certain patterns according to the types they belong to, tend to behave approximately in the same manner in the same circumstances.

Carl Jung, an eminent psychiatrist, was the first one in the modern era to have categorised personalities. He said people can be classified into 'Introverts' and 'Extroverts'. Introverts, he said are quiet, withdrawn and 'seethe internally' when confronted by a stressful situation. They try and tackle the issue at a personal level and not seek the help of others. 'Extroverts' on the other hand are aggressive, talkative and communicate issues with people around. They need the company of other people to feel complete. Under stressful circumstances, they tend to open up with others and seek solutions to their own problems.

Friedman and Rosanmann in recent times categorised personality types of individuals into 'Type A' and 'Type B' depending on whether he or she reacts to stress aggressively or in a subdued manner. Some of the traits on which this categorisation was done are illustrated in the following table.

Profiles of Type A and Type B Personalities (Ref 2)

Type A	Type B
Always Time Conscious	Not concerned about time
Walks, talks, eats rapidly	Relaxed, fun loving, calm
Does two things at one time	No pressing dead lines
Aggressive	Mild Mannered
Obsessed with numbers	Never in a hurry
Quantity oriented	Quality Conscious
Competitive	Cooperative

It is found that Type A personalities are more prone to stress induced disorders such as high blood pressure and even cardiac arrest while Type B persons are less prone to these diseases. Again, this is, in a way, relative and situation dependent.

In reality, individuals are a combination of Type A and B, more of A and less of B or vice versa. These are Type AB personalities. They have the positive qualities and the negative qualities of both types.

What is important for us to realise and be aware that we can swing either way towards both types and we need to become more conscious of our personality traits and be willing to adjust and correct in order to cope with stress.

In the next chapter, we will deal elaborately with the methods of identifying warning signs and symptoms of various natures before we move on to other sections of this book in to ways and means of coping with stress, eventually winning over them to emerge victorious.

Chapter - 4

Symptoms of Stress – Warning Signs

"The mind can't delete what the heart won't let go of."
–Peggy Toney Horton, Stop the World and Get Off

As discussed in the earlier chapters, all kinds of stress are not bad. Depending upon the nature of the stress some are classified positive or eustress while some are classified as distress. The frequency of occurrence of stress and the severity of the stress on a given occasion also matters.

The personality of the individual which we will discuss in greater detail later on in this book, classified as 'Type A', 'Type B' or 'Type AB' for aggressive, mild and mixed types of personality traits in individuals and their ability to cope has a role in deciding the way people will react, respond and manage stress which has consequences on their body, mind, emotions and health (Ref 2).

All said and done, wrongful effects of stress will result in physiological and psychological changes in the body which if left unchecked and ignored could result in discomforts to the mind and body and in the long run, lead to diseases and even death, finally.

There are early warning signs of stress and prolonged symptoms which can be classified into four types (Ref 2, 3, 4):

1. Physical signs or symptoms
2. Emotional signs or symptoms
3. Cognitive or perceptual symptoms
4. Behavioural symptoms

Let us look at some examples of general early warning signs in an individual which indicate that he or she is getting prone to the attack of stress and subsequent serious consequences of stress if the warning signs are ignored and not attended to or looked into.

Early Warning Signs of Stress

- Menstrual problems
- Speech difficulties
- High levels of impatience
- Headaches
- Infertility
- Ulcers
- Nail biting
- Grinding teeth
- Low blood sugar
- High blood sugar
- Sleeplessness
- Tired but can't sleep
- Sudden weight loss
- Sudden weight gain
- Low blood pressure
- High blood pressure
- Lack of coordination
- Repeated influenza
- Repeated colds
- Muscle aches
- Hair loss
- Chest pain
- Forgetfulness
- Nervous talking
- Lower back pain
- Loss of appetite
- Increased appetite
- High cholesterol
- High triglycerides

- Excessive fatigue
- Gastric disturbance
- Withdrawal from social life.

These early warning signs should alert an individual that things are not going the right way and so caution needs to be exercised to cope with and preserve health. Classification of prolonged stress symptoms, analysis and action is required once the early warning signs are ignored and the individual becomes stress ridden. Obviously a lot of knowledge regarding stress and its management is warranted in the individual to become aware, understand, know, combat and conquer the ill effects of stress and the diseases which stem from the neglect of the symptoms.

The following pages list out the physical, emotional, cognitive and behavioural symptoms of stress in order to enable the reader to become more aware and knowledgeable in managing stress.

Physical Signs and Symptoms of Stress

- Increased heart rate
- Pounding heart
- Elevated blood pressure
- Sweaty palms
- Tightness of the chest, neck, jaw, and back muscles
- Headache
- Diarrhea
- Constipation
- Urinary hesitancy
- Trembling
- Twitching
- Stuttering and other speech difficulties
- Nausea
- Vomiting
- Sleep disturbances
- Fatigue
- Shallow breathing

- Dryness of the mouth or throat
- Susceptibility to minor illness
- Cold hands
- Itching
- Being easily startled
- Chronic pain, and
- Dysponesis.

Emotional Signs and Symptoms of Stress

- Irritability
- Angry outbursts
- Hostility
- Depression
- Jealously
- Restlessness
- Withdrawal
- Anxiousness
- Diminished initiative
- Feelings of unreality or over-alertness
- Reduction of personal involvement with others
- Lack of interest
- Tendency to cry
- Being critical of others
- Self-deprecation
- Nightmares
- Impatience
- Decreased perception of positive
- Experience opportunities
- Narrowed focus
- Obsessive rumination
- Reduced self-esteem
- Insomnia
- Changes in eating habits and
- Weakened positive emotional response reflexes.

Cognitive/Perceptual Signs and Symptoms of Stress

- Forgetfulness
- Preoccupation
- Blocking
- Blurred vision
- Errors in judging distance
- Diminished or exaggerated fantasy life
- Reduced creativity
- Lack of concentration
- Diminished productivity
- Lack of attention to detail
- Orientation to the past
- Decreased psychomotor reactivity and coordination
- Attention deficit
- Disorganisation of thought
- Negative self-esteem
- Diminished sense of meaning in life
- Lack of control/need for too much control
- Negative self-statements and negative evaluation of experiences.

Behavioural Signs and Symptoms of Stress

- Increased smoking
- Aggressive behaviours (such as driving - road rage, etc.)
- Increased alcohol or drug use
- Carelessness
- Under-eating
- Over-eating
- Withdrawal
- Listlessness
- Hostility
- Accident-proneness
- Nervous laughter

- Compulsive behaviour, and
- Impatience.

Signs of Stress in the Workplace Executive Stress and Symptoms

Extensive research by experts like Judy Marshall and Cary Cooper reveal that middle level managers in organisations, corporates of any kind experience more physiological and psychological stress than senior managers or junior executives. The reasons attributed are:

1. Time pressures
2. Job responsibilities
3. Problems of managing people
4. Less or no authority with more responsibility
5. Worries regarding career advancement.

The senior managers get most of the work done by exerting pressures on the middle level managers with deadlines and work requirements while the same cannot be done by the middle level manager with junior persons under them who are much less experienced and skilled. Cooper and Marshall have identified the following six different kinds of job related stress for managers in a work place, which are:

1. *Factors intrinsic to the job:* These are aspects like working conditions, work load, quantitative and qualitative restrictions, excessive travel, too many decisions, tight deadlines and time pressures.
2. *Role in the organisation:* The factors include things like role ambiguity, role conflicts and role responsibilities. Role ambiguity implies lack of clarity about the goals, expectations of people around, nature scope and responsibilities of the job. Role conflict would mean the conflicting expectations of people with whom one is interacting, not willing to do what is expected to be done and so on. Responsibility for people is found to be more stressful for many people that responsibility for the job.
3. *Relationships at work:* These include relationship with colleagues, relationship with superiors and subordinates.

Factors like low trust and low supportiveness and group morale and cohesiveness can be reasons for generation of excess stress.

4. *Career disappointments:* Factors like not being promoted on time, being passed over by juniors for promotion, not being recognised for performance etc., are stressors which affect an individual at work. These can be very debilitating causing health loss for the person in the long run.
5. *Organisational structure and climate:* Poor communication structures within the organisation, line-staff conflicts, buraucracy, too many levels between the top and bottom hampering grievance redressal, poor performance assessment systems without feedbacks and training and development opportunities are some of the reasons why employees in an organisation may get stressed out and consequently perform less while losing health too.
6. *Extra-organisational stressors:* These can be factors like social, technological changes, financial and family problems, relocation and so on.

In an organisational environment, individuals experience stresses in an increasing magnitude in different stages. They need to become aware of these stages if they have to prevent or cope with them in a rational way. These different stages are mentioned below.

Stress Arousal Stage

- Persistent irritability and anxiety
- Bruxism and/or insomnia
- Occasional forgetfulness and/or inability to concentrate.

Stress Resistance Stage

- Absenteeism or tardiness for work
- Tired and fatigued for no reason
- Procrastination and indecision
- Social withdrawal with cynicism
- Resentful, indifferent, defiant
- Increased use of coffee, alcohol, tobacco, etc.

Severe Exhaustion Stage

- Chronic sadness or depression
- Chronic mental and physical fatigue
- Chronic stress related illnesses (headache, stomach ache, bowel problems, etc.
- Isolation, withdrawal, self-destructive thoughts.

By becoming aware of the symptoms mentioned above, the individual can understand the stage in which he or she is and take appropriate steps to combat and resolve the health, performance and career decisions one needs to take. It is very surprising to know that many or most of us are not tuned to job-stress effects on us before it takes over our lives completely not only in the work place but also in our personal lives and at home.

Recent Research Findings: Stress and Aging

Recent research results suggest that long-term exposure to adrenal stress hormones may boost brain aging in later life.

Writing in the journal Nature Neuroscience, scientists at the University of Kentucky in Lexington looked at the results of memory tests taken by elderly patients with high levels of the stress hormone cortisol, released by adrenal glands when the body is stressed. That high-level group scored lower than others with reduced levels of the hormone, researchers say.

The level of hormone released apparently affects the total volume of the brain's hippocampus — a major source of recall and memory function — in later life. Those with high levels had a hippocampus volume 14 per cent less than those with lower levels, researchers found.

The study results suggest, "chronic stress may accelerate hippocampal deterioration," said the researchers.

Chapter - 5

The Effects of Stress on Systems in the Body

"Breathing is our participation with the cosmic dance. When our breath is in harmony, cosmos nourishes us in every sense."

– *Amit Ray, Beautify your Breath - Beautify your Life*

We have seen in the earlier chapter and discussed in a very elaborate manner as to how stress in an individual manifests itself and begins to show early warning signs followed by severe symptoms which can be physical, psychological, cognitive, emotional or behavioural in nature. These are essentially responses of the body and mind to the stress stimulus from outside.

What we have not considered so far are the consequences when due to prolonged stress situation, the internal thoughts and emotions start getting distorted and the impact spreads to the person's whole being.

Under such conditions, people start experiencing a sense of being overwhelmed physically and emotionally. They experience intense levels of anxiety and tension. Thinking gets disorganised. The normal fight flee responses get disoriented and mixed up. Defence mechanisms within the body and mind cannot cope, neurosis sets in eventually the individual may become 'psychotic' mentally and behaviourally. Intervention from medical and psychiatrists may be required. In fact, the situation can so get out of control that the individual may have to be interned in asylums meant to treat such disorders for long periods and still the recovery may not be complete.

Abnormal Reactions to Stress (Ref 3, 4, 6, 9)

As we mentioned in the foregoing paragraph, when severe stress prolongs for long periods of time in an individual, the person experiences intense anxiety and personality disorders begin to appear in him. In fact, with persistent stress the individual begins to feel that the core or the essence of his very being and personality feel totally threatened. The individual mentally become unconscious of the 'self' and begins to 'delude' and 'hallucinate'.

Neurotic and Psychotic Disorders

Neurotic disorders are sustained, persistent and compulsive behaviours. They are disabling in nature, in thoughts and emotions. They are debilitating to health and personality of the individual. Unconscious conflicts come to the surface and result in unwanted anxieties in a person afflicted neurotically. Neurotic disorders include eating disorders, drug and alcohol abuse, mood disorders, anxiety oriented disorders, memory oriented disorders like ȃmnesia, hypochondria and so on. Obsessive compulsive behaviours fall within the gambit of neurotic behaviours.

Psychotic disorders are nothing but extensions of neurotic disorders taken to the very extreme of the behavioural spectrum. These are the behaviours exhibited by individuals under very severe, sustained distress situations. Prolonged anxiety and stress lead an individual to a disconnect with reality. The individual may show symptoms of delusions, illusions and hallucinations totally unrelated to the real situations around him or her. Disturbed emotions, affective cognitions and extreme behaviours which can even be very violent at times are common in psychosis. Some of the main categorisations in psychotic disorders happen to be Schizophrenia (split personality), paranoia and mania.

The author does not wish to delve deeper into this topic on mental disorders, since it is in the realm of specialist mental experts like the psychologist and psychiatrists. It will be sufficient to say that unchecked stress can lead one to total mental breakdowns such as the ones discussed above.

In the following section gives a list of the bad effects of stress on all the physiological systems of the body.

The Effects of Stress on Systems in the Body

Central Nervous System

Anxiety, depression, and fatigue.

Cardiovascular System

Impaired heart function; can cause angina

Constriction of the peripheral blood vessels, thereby raising blood pressure.

Digestive System

Stomach upsets, even ulcers

Diarrhea

Gastritis

Peptic ulcers

Irritable Bowel Syndrome

Colitis

Canker sores in the mouth.

Respiratory System

Asthma.

Musculoskeletal System

Tension in skeletal muscles and joints, leading to backache and muscular aches and pains

Predisposition to arthritis; degenerative diseases such as rheumatoid arthritis.

Immune System

Weakened defenses, with lowered resistance to infections

Viral illnesses (often due to a depleted immune defense system)

Allergies

Malignant cell changes; cancer.

Endocrine System

Menstrual disorders

Thyroid disorders (underactive, overactive, thyroiditis)

Adrenal hypofunction

Reproductive System

Infertility

Premature ejaculation

Impotence.

Skin

Eczema

Psoriasis

Rashes.

General

Tissue degeneration

Acceleration of aging process.

We can see very clearly from the above descriptions that all the life sustaining systems of the body and within it are totally affected by elongated stress. Irreversible damage occurs and sometimes the situation becomes life threatening. The reverse argument will be, then, that when all these or any of these disorders are encountered by the body, one has to infer and understand that the root cause can be severe stress sustained by oneself for long periods. If unattended and in fact, remedied, the situation will become irreversible resulting in even death of an individual.

In the following sections of the book, we will see how we can employ different methods and adopt different habits in our daily lives so that we can effectively deal with stress and its bad effects in our lives. The author goes on to explain how we can combine many of these techniques in an integrated manner so as to come victorious in our battle with stress and lead a happy, healthy life. This in the very purpose of this book.

Chapter - 6

Coping With Stress: Remedial Actions

"Feeling good about yourself is the best sleeping pill of all."
–Annika Sorensen, Take Stress from Chaos to Calm

We have learnt a lot about the origins of stress, its nature and ways of identifying the presence of stress in individuals in the previous chapters. Now, it is time for us to understand the ways of coping with it in order to remedy the ill effects of it on our mind and body.

Before we get into the techniques or better still, the skills involved in handling stress, the author would like to share a critical thought going on in his mind, with the reader for his comprehension of the challenges involved in managing stress effectively.

The word coping is used in stress management because stress is very real in all situations in life and is difficult to completely eliminate in life. Whether stress is positive or negative, i.e., whether it is eustress or distress, stress leaves its mark on our mind and body forever. When it becomes negative and distressful, the damages done to our systems are more pronounced and detrimental to health.

There is nothing like a total blissful way of combating stress, as the spiritualists claim, when they talk about prayer or meditation. The best we can achieve, the author believes, will be to minimise the bad effects of stress and maximise or optimise the benefits by using all the skills necessary and the appropriate knowledge to acquire the skills. Hence, we have the concept of 'Coping'. Yes, when we cope well with the challenges of managing mind and body, we can say, we have emerged victorious. But, it is a conditional situation. It needs a constant battle throughout life with all the attention and skill, in order that we cope, win, gain happiness, health and wisdom.

Remedial Action to Control Stress (Ref 3, 4, 5, 9, 10)

The actions we can take or the methods we adopt to cope with stress can be very broadly classified into three major categories. They are:

- Changing Our Thinking
- Changing Our Behaviour
- Changing Our Life Style.

All the techniques we are going to discuss, including methods like yoga, meditation and prayer, fall in to these broad categories and hence, the author believes that more divisions are not necessary. This approach makes the task of understanding stress management fairly straight forward and easy.

Changing Our Thinking

In this section, we are going to discuss in detail two techniques of making our thinking positive under all circumstances. They are:

- Reframing
- Positive Thinking

Before we begin to go in to the details of these methods, let us try and understand some of the basic facts about how behaviour gets initiated from our thoughts, how it sustains and how it can be controlled and ended through thoughts if ending behaviour is warranted in certain situations as it may lead to consequences undesirable and hence stressful.

Reframing

Reframing is a technique used to change the way we look at stressful things and events in order that we feel better and less threatened about them. The key to reframing is to recognise that there are many ways to interpret the same situation. A good example that makes this concept easy to understand is that of a person looking at a glass that is half empty and interprets that it is half full which is equally true. The trick is to learn to get rid of negative thoughts or feelings under stressful situations and looking at the positive side of the same situation for not having expanded to a worse or even the worst possible level. It is more a way we perceive and interpret than the situation per se.

There are three simple things you can do.

- Spend more time focusing on the positive things in your life, that is, accentuate the positive.
- Spend less time thinking negatively - Eliminate the negative.
- Enjoy each moment - Latch on to the affirmative.

For example, if you have got into an accident, you may thank God that you have escaped with only minor injuries. You could have been killed, or worse, you could have been maimed – lost eyes, feet, hands, etc. You could have been paralyzed. You could have been in a comma and become a vegetable.

Another way to rationalise is to believe in coincidences and what it can do. The author would like to share with the reader that earlier in his career in corporates, he switched from automobile industry to software which resulted in many benefits including financial, career and life, when suddenly there was a boom in the software sector in India which stays unabated even now.

If you are religious or believe in spirituality, that can be a great coping mechanism. For example, religion teaches us that everything happens for a purpose and it is the will of God. You just leave the things to God to straighten out. The result is that your brain does not have to pump out adrenaline to your bloodstream constantly. You feel relaxed. There is no long-term stress any more.

Positive Thinking

Avoid negative thoughts of powerlessness, dejection, failure, and despair. Chronic stress makes us vulnerable to negative suggestion. Learn to focus on positives.

- Focus on your strengths
- Learn from the stress you are under
- Look for opportunities in the stressful situation
- Seek out the positive – make a change.

Here is one way to get out of the destructive negative thinking habits. All possible situations we face can be classified into two categories:

One: Situations where we can do something about to change the outcome. In this case, don't just sit there and worry about it. Go ahead and take care of it. You have control. Procrastination is the root cause for many stressful episodes.

Second: Situations where you have no control on the outcome. In this case sitting and worrying will not make any difference on the outcome. So, don't worry about it. Let the situation resolve by itself; you cannot do anything about this anyway.

A great thinker talked about how our culture teaches us to dwell on the high stress activities. He gave this example: Two Arabs took their Mercedes car out for a spin in the desert. Although there probably was not another car in the 10-mile radius, these two guys managed to have a head-on collision. Now, if this happened in the USA or many other parts of the world, the drivers will be getting out of the car and showering each other with abuses, threats and remind the other person how stupid he was to cause the accident. What did the Arabs do after they had their cars totaled? They rush out of their cars, run to each other; hugs and say, "This is great! Allah, you wanted us to meet. Thank you so much."

Spiritually speaking, the key to moving on is forgiveness,-of self and others. Although it is a waste of energy to worry about future events over which we have no control, it is human nature to do so. Plan and prioritize as best you can, and then be easy on yourself. The future hasn't happened, and the past is not going to happen again. In the words of a great man, "Be here now." You can start by recognising and accepting when a situation is beyond your control.

And keep on practicing. Pythagoras said, "Choose always the way that seems the best, however rough it may be. Custom will soon render it easy and agreeable." Just as patterns and habits can trap us when we let them, we can make them our well-worn path to happiness and satisfaction.

The "Serenity Prayer", by a very great theologian the world produced in the past, reflects this idea so well. It reads like this:

> "God, grant me the serenity to accept the things I cannot change, courage to change the things I can, and the wisdom to know the difference, living one day at a time, enjoying one moment at a time, accepting hardships as the pathway to peace."

Difference between Reframing and Positive Thinking

It is necessary to underline the difference between reframing and positive thinking. In fact, the dividing lines between the two processes are thin and subtle.

Reframing is a methodology of thinking one can adopt when already a stressful, negative event or a situation has occurred. One has a choice to mull over the negative consequences and get depressed or the option to look at the situation in a new positive manner, reinterpret or reframe so that the negative impact of the situation does not affect the mind and one is ready to learn and cope with the consequences and eventually come out victorious.

Positive thinking on the other hand does not have to wait for a negative situation to occur. As and when the mind switches between a cluster of positive and negative thoughts, one trains oneself to think about all imagined thoughts in a positive way, strategize, plan and develop a mental attitude strong enough to bring the plans into positive actions. Positive thinking is more futuristic and action oriented. The practitioner of positive thinking develops a strong will to plan and make things happen. A positive thinking person is an optimist and a believer, not a pessimist and a loser.

One can use both techniques of thinking in a mixed manner, depending upon the events and situations he or she faces in life and learn to be comfortable at all times. After all, the objective is to be stress-free under all circumstances, succeed and win.

Chapter - 7

Changing Our Behaviour

"If you don't want stress, detach yourself from the stressors"

–Genica JC

In the previous chapter, we dealt with one of the most important steps in coping with stress, namely, thinking. We said that reframing and positive thinking are two methods by which one can interpret stress, its causes and consequences in a positive manner, in order that we can deal effectively with it and emerge successful.

The psychologists and even the spiritualists admit that all human behaviour, attitudes and the belief systems emanate from the thoughts we generate at the instance of a stimulus or the occurrence of a life's event. How we react and respond to any new situation or a situation we have encountered earlier but re-appears, depends on the way our minds generate the thoughts to begin with which proliferates into actions later on depending on what we decide to do with the thoughts so generated by ourselves.

In this chaper, we wish to discuss in detail, some of the ways in which we can look upon the behaviours we exhibit when encountering stressful situations or stressors in life and modify them in order to deal with the stress generated. The following few methods are suggested.

Changing Our Behaviour

- Being Assertive
- Getting Organised/Time Management
- Ventilation

- Humour
- Diversion and Distraction.

We will deal with each of these techniques of managing stress through behaviour one by one in the following sections.

Being Assertive

Learn to be assertive. Non-assertiveness allows others to walk all over you. You surrender the control of the situation to others. Being assertive means standing up for your personal rights and expressing your thoughts, feelings and beliefs directly, honestly and spontaneously in ways that don't infringe on the rights of others. Assertive people respect themselves and others. They take responsibility for their actions and choices. In case of failure, they will get disappointed; but their self-confidence remains intact. Expressing negative feelings at the appropriate time avoids the buildup of resentment. This will help you manage your stress more successfully.

An example will illustrate this point. An elderly patient, Lissie, was very frustrated because she had no time to do anything for herself. It seemed, she was looking after others all the time. After participating in the assertiveness training, Lissie started analysing what activities gave her the most happiness. She came to the conclusion that a Tuesday morning bridge game she played with her friends was one of them. One Tuesday, Lissie was preparing to host the card game, when the telephone rang. It was her daughter. The daughter had a very important meeting to go to that morning; but her babysitter called in sick. She had no one to take care of her son. She wanted to know if she could bring her son to Lissie's home so that she can go to her meeting she could not miss?

Lissie felt her pulse going up. She was expecting her friends at any moment. It was too late to cancel in the card game. Having the grandson around would prevent her from enjoying the game. It would also be distracting and annoying to the other members of the team. On the other hand, what kind of mom is she, if she were to refuse to help her daughter when she needed her? Then Lissie thought of her assertiveness training.

Lissie asked the daughter, "Why don't you take your son to the daycare centre?" There is one very close to her home. The daughter replied that she was broke and did not have any money to pay for the daycare. Lissie offered to loan her the money so that she could take her son to the daycare centre. The situation was resolved to everyone's satisfaction.

Getting Organised/Time Management

One of the most common causes of stress is being disorganised at work or at home. Here are some tips to get organised:

Keep a Diary

Write lists of tasks to accomplish, prioritize them and schedule when you will complete them.

Writing down objectives, duties and activities helps to make them more tangible and do-able. Having a schedule also helps you provide the facts when your boss asks you to perform unreasonable tasks. They may have no idea that you are overwhelmed with work and the additional responsibilities cannot be accomplished unless something else goes. Again, prioritizing tasks helps you to minimise the stressful situations.

Make a List and Prioritize

So many projects, so little time. To beat stress, you have to learn to prioritize. At the start of each day, pick the single most important task to complete, then finish it. If you're a person who makes to-do lists, never write one with more than five items. That way, you're more likely to get all the things done, and you'll feel a greater sense of accomplishment and control. Then you can go ahead and make a second five-item list. While you're at it, make a list of things that you can delegate to co-workers and family members.

Learn to Say No When Appropriate

Sometimes you have to learn to draw the line. Stressed-out people often can't assert themselves. Instead of saying 'I don't want to do this' or 'I need some help,' they do it all themselves. Then they have even more to do.

Give Your Boss a Choice

Say 'I'd really like to take this on, but I can't do that without giving up something else. Which of these things would you like me to do?' Most bosses can take the hint. The same strategy works at home, with your spouse, children, relatives and friends. If you have trouble saying no, start small. Tell your hubby to make his own sandwich. Or tell your daughter to find another ride home from volleyball practice.

Pad Your Schedule

Realise that nearly everything will take longer than you anticipate. By allotting yourself enough time to accomplish a task, you cut back on anxiety. In general, if meeting deadlines is a problem, always give yourself 20 per cent more time than you think you need to do the task.

Other Tips on Time Management

Look at the way you do things. Are you a perfectionist? If so, try to decide which tasks truly require meticulous attention to detail and which can be done casually.

Make a realistic list of what you need to accomplish in a given day, with the most important things at the top. Tackle them one at a time, and don't start a second until you have finished the first.

Plan your day to include work breaks which physically or mentally take you away from the office. Try not to bring office work home.

When you have several things to accomplish, set priorities and postpone less important tasks. Learn to delegate matters that cannot be put off. Deal with concerns on a day-at-a-time basis.

Control the timing of stressful events. Try not to make major decisions when you are overtired or anxious.

Ventilation

People who keep things for themselves without sharing with their friends or loved ones carry a considerable and unnecessary burden. Share your problems and concern with others. Develop a support system of relatives, colleagues or friends to talk to when you are upset or worried. When you are frustrated write it down. After you have vented the frustration, destroy the writing so that it is forgotten. Rereading the journal will reawaken the frustration and anger. So, do not keep it.

Seek social support. Studies have shown that close, positive relationships with others facilitate good health and morale. One reason for this is that support from family and friends serves as a buffer to cushion the impact of stressful events. Talking out problems and expressing tensions can be incredibly helpful. If things really get bad, seek help from a therapist, counsellor, or clergyman.

Transference

Hold a rock in your hand and envision all your stress and anxiety flowing through your fingers and palm into the rock. After you "feel" that the bad stuff has been transferred to the rock, throw the rock away or bury it or toss it into running water. You can also "wash" the rock and rinse away the "bad stuff" and reuse the rock.

Humour Therapy

Humour is a wonderful stress-reducer and antidote to upsets. It is clinically proven to be effective in combating stress, although the exact mechanism is not known. Experts say a good laugh relaxes tense muscles, speeds more oxygen into your system and lowers your blood pressure. So tune into your favourite sitcom on television. Read a funny book. Call a friend and chuckle for a few minutes. It even helps to force a laugh once in a while. You'll find your stress melting away almost instantly. Americans were attracted to humour from the stories of Norman Cousins, who had successfully overcome cancer by watching comedy shows on television. These days, there are organised humour meetings even in places like India where laughing in public is not considered good manner.

Dr Lee Berk and fellow researcher Dr Stanley Tan at Loma Linda University School of Medicine, has produced carefully controlled studies showing that the experience of laughter lowers serum cortisol levels, increases the amount of activated T lymphocytes, increases the number and activity of natural killer cells, and increases the number of T cells that have helper/ suppresser receptors. In short, laughter stimulates the immune system, off-setting the immuno-suppressive effects of stress.

We know that, during stress, the adrenal gland releases corticosteroids (quickly converted to cortisol in the blood stream) and that elevated levels of these have an immunosuppressive effect. Berk's research demonstrates that laughter can lower cortisol levels and thereby protect our immune system.

The emotions and moods we experience directly affect our immune system. A sense of humour allows us to perceive and appreciate the incongruities of life and provides moments of joy and delight. These positive emotions can create neurochemical changes that will buffer the immunosuppressive effects of stress.

In his book, *'Stress without Distress,'* Selye suggested that a person's interpretation of stress is not dependent solely on an external event, but also depends upon the perception of the event and the meaning he or she gives it. So, how you look at a situation determines if you will respond to it as threatening or challenging.

Humor gives us a different perspective on our problems. If we can make light out of the situation, it is no longer threatening to us. We already discounted its effect. With such an attitude of detachment, we feel a sense of self-protection and control in our environment. Bill Cosby is fond of saying, "If you can laugh at it, you can survive it."

It's sometimes difficult to force a laugh in tense situations. But that's precisely when you need it most. One trick for finding humour in the worst of situations is to blow things absolutely, ridiculously out of proportion. When your scenario reaches the point of absurdity, you begin to smile. The situation is put in perspective. Now you can calm down.

A belly laugh is really good for you. It relieves muscular tension, improves breathing, and regulates the heart beat. Watch comedy shows and laugh. Or attend comedy shows. Read comics or humour books. Share funny episodes with your spouse so that both can relieve stress as well improve communication between the two of you.

Diversion and Distraction

Take a break away from the situations or tasks that are the source of your stress and frustration. Take a vacation or a short walk. This does not solve the root cause. But, it takes away from the source of stress so that you can "catch your breath." It also gives you an opportunity to think about the situation more objectively and may even help you to resolve the situation when looked through a different perspective.

Doctors agree that being physically active—walking, stretching, even working in the garden-is a high-power stress buster.

Stretch Yourself

Stretching can help you feel more peaceful and relaxed. As you stretch, imagine the tension leaving your back, neck and other muscles as you gently push them to their comfortable limit.

Walk it off. Walking may be the oldest stress reducer of all. Studies at California State University have shown significant reductions in tension after walks lasting only several minutes. A study by Florida's State Department of Health and Rehabilitative Services found that participants in an eight week walking programme were able to reduce the stress they felt at work by 30 per cent. Walking not only can provide a needed escape from tension, it also may increase the body's production of mood-elevating brain chemicals called endorphins.

Gardening

Gardening is a natural, stress-releasing activity without the contrivance and inconvenience of working out at a health club. Experts suggest that gardening takes our minds off the unsolvable problems we confront every day. It gives us work to do where we can see progress from minute to minute. In that sense it works like meditation; It takes your mind away from stressful thoughts.

Conclusion

Changing behaviour as a technique for stress management is easier than changing thinking as discussed in the earlier chapter. The main reason for this is that behaviour is seen in the everyday actions of human beings. One can observe one's own behaviour or ask others to observe and give a feedback. Behaviour is learnt from people through cognition or imitation. So, to change one's behavior, one has to indulge in a repetitive new kind of behaviour for a while, say about a month or so and then it becomes habitual and is remembered by the mind and stored in its memory.

A certain amount of will power in developing new habits is a must during this change period of a month so that subsequently, the new pattern of behaviour becomes automatic or spontaneous when the same circumstances or stimuli are encountered. Changing thinking patterns on the other hand is more challenging, since at any instance a large number of thoughts are generated by the human mind. So, identifying negative patterns requires a lot of reflection and attention within in order to catch the negativity in thinking as and when it occurs.

We will discuss this method in more detail when we analyse techniques such as yoga, meditation and prayer in the next chapter on changing life styles for coping with and overcoming the ill effects of stress on the human body, mind and spirit.

Chapter - 8

Changing Our Life Style

"Holding on to the past will hold you down in life. Learn from it but move on." – *Jonathan Anthony Burkett*

Before we begin, we need to understand the difference between the words 'Changing Behaviour' and 'Changing Life Style'. We know from psychological sciences around us that behind each human behaviour which is visible to the naked eye, there is a thought process and an intention. Each of these intentions are driven by mental 'Attitudes' which reflect the state of mind or the mental positioning an individual takes while generating those intentions.

Attitudes of individuals have emanated from the deeply held belief and value systems which they have acquired from the culture, traditions and the family backgrounds they belong to and partially through the education and life experiences they gathered during the process of growth.

Lifestyle changes (Ref 3, 4), hence, would imply an entire shift in thinking and behaviour starting at the grass root level starting from belief and value systems held by people, from the very core. When one makes these kinds of changes, not only the behaviour changes, but it changes for good and stays changed. So, life style changes for improved mind and body conditioning can be very beneficial so far as managing or coping with stress is concerned.

The following sections of his book discuss some of the life style changes one can adopt while encountering distressful events or situations in life, which can be of a prolonged nature and hence can cause permanent damage to the mind and body. The consequences of not combating the effects of some of the stresses can be fatal and so life style changes are not only worth considering but sometimes become unavoidable and vital.

The following methods of modifying life styles are going to be discussed in this chapter to give the reader a very broad understanding of the width of changes one can bring about in the manner in which one lives and the possibilities of changes one can accomplish in order to lead a better, healthier and hence a longer life with more quality. The subjects we will be covering are:

- Diet
- Exercises
- Drink Water
- Deep Breathing
- Nature Walks and Imagery
- Hydrotherapy: A Warm, Hot Bath
- Music Therapy
- Sleep
- Yoga
- Meditation
- Prayer

Out of all these life style changes we are going to suggest for coping with and eventually winning over stress, we will be discussing the last three in the list, namely, yoga, meditation and prayer under the heading spirituality in the next chapter. The reason, the author feels strongly, is that a deeper understanding of the purpose of life is required by any individual, in order that he can master the art or the science of living well.

Without bringing any religious biases in to these spiritual techniques meant for an integrated health and personality, the author proposes to share a lot of well researched, already available, scientific knowledge in spirituality for the benefit of any reader regardless of whether he calls himself a believer or non-believer.

The intentions of the author are entirely neutral, value adding and not aimed at influencing the reader with regard to any particular religious views or sentiments. The author feels compelled to emphasise this attitude and intention of his in very clear terms, before you read on further.

Let us continue our journey in stress management, with regard to life style changes, in the following sections:

Diet

A well balanced diet is crucial in preserving health and helping to reduce stress. Certain foods and drinks act as powerful stimulants to the body and hence are a direct cause of stress. This stimulation, although quite pleasurable in the short term, may be quite harmful in the long run. We will look at a few of them:

Caffeine

This is found in coffee, tea, chocolate, coke, etc. It causes the release of adrenaline, thus increasing the level of stress. When taken in moderation, coffee can increase your alertness, increased activity in the muscles, nervous system and heart. Consuming too much caffeine has the same effect as long term stress. It is suggested that there is a link between caffeine intake and high blood pressure and high cholesterol levels.

Be careful in reducing the coffee or caffeine consumption. Cutting it off abruptly can result in your experiencing withdrawal symptoms. Reduce the consumption slowly over a period of time.

Alcohol

Like caffeine, taken in moderation, alcohol is a very useful drug. It has been shown to benefit cardiovascular system. Alcohol is a major cause of stress. The irony of the situation is that most people take to drinking as way to combat stress. But, in actuality, they make it worse by consuming alcohol. Alcohol and stress, in combination, are quite deadly.

Alcohol stimulates the secretion of adrenaline resulting in the problems such as nervous tension, irritability and insomnia. Excess alcohol will increase the fat deposits in the heart and decrease the immune function. Alcohol also limits the ability of the liver to remove toxins from the body. During stress, the body produces several toxins such as hormones. In the absence of its filtering by the liver, these toxins continue to circulate through the body resulting in serious damage.

Smoking

Many people use cigarettes as a coping mechanism. In the short-term, smoking seems to relieve stress. But in the long-term smoking is very harmful. Its disadvantages far outweigh its short-term benefits. Cigarette smoking is shown to be responsible for a variety of cancers, hypertension, respiratory illness and heart disease.

Sugar

Sugar has no essential nutrients. It provides a short-term boost of energy through the body, resulting possibly in the exhaustion of the adrenal glands. This can result in irritability, poor concentration, and depression. High sugar consumption puts a severe load on the pancreas. There is increasing possibility of developing diabetes.

Keep your blood sugar constant. Do not use sugar as a "pick me up."

Salt

Salt increases the blood pressure, deplete adrenal glands, and causes emotional instability. Use a salt substitute that has potassium rather than sodium. Avoid junk foods high in salt such as bacon, ham, pickles, sausage, etc.

Fat

Avoid the consumption of foods rich in saturated fats. Fats cause obesity and put unnecessary stress on the cardiovascular system. High fat is believed to cause breast, colon and prostate cancers.

Eat a Meal High in Carbohydrates

Carbohydrates trigger release of the brain neurotransmitter serotonin, which soothes you. Good sources of carbohydrates include rice, pasta, potatoes, breads, air-popped popcorn and low-cal cookies. Experts suggest that the carbohydrates present in a baked potato or a cup of spaghetti or white rice is enough to relieve the anxiety of a stressful day.

Eat Food High in Fiber

Stress result in cramps and constipation. Eat more fiber to keep your digestive system moving. Your meal should provide at least

25 grams of fiber per day. Fruits, vegetables and grains are excellent sources of fiber. For breakfast, eat whole fruits instead of just juice, and whole-grain cereals and fiber-fortified muffins.

Eat More Vegetables

Your brain's production of Serotonin, is sensitive to your diet. Eating more vegetables can increase your brain's Serotonin production. This increase is due to improved absorption of the amino acid L-Tryptophan. (Vegetables contain the natural, safe, form of L Tryptophan.) Meats contain natural L-Tryptophan also, but when you eat meat, the L-Tryptophan has to compete with so many other amino acids for absorption that the L-Tryptophan loses out. The net result is that you get better absorption of L-Tryptophan when you eat vegetables.

Foods to Eat

Whole grains promote the production of the brain neurotransmitter serotonin, which increases your sense of well being.

Green, yellow, and orange vegetables are all rich in minerals, vitamins, and phytochemicals, which boost immune response and protect against disease.

Foods to Avoid

Coffee and other caffeinated beverages: If you are currently addicted to coffee, drink black tea; it has less than a third of the caffeine of coffee, and none of the harmful oils.

Fried foods and foods rich in fat are very immune depressing, especially when stress is doing that, as well.

Reduce animal foods. High-protein foods elevate brain levels of dopamine and norepinephrine, both of which are associated with higher levels of anxiety and stress.

You should also take a good multi-vitamin and mineral preparation.

Exercise

Research has shown that physical exercise is the best tension reliever. It is a very important remedy for stress. Nothing eases stress more than exercise. Exercise, when property done, gives your body time to operate in the efficiency mode.

Physically, exercise improves your cardiovascular functions by strengthening and enlarging the heart, causing greater elasticity of the blood vessels, increasing oxygen throughout your body, and lowering your blood levels of fats such as cholesterol and triglycerides. All of this, of course, means less chance of developing heart conditions, strokes, or high blood pressure.

Mentally, exercise provides an outlet for negative emotions such as frustration, anger, and irritability, thereby promoting a more positive mood and outlook. Exercise improves mood by producing positive biochemical changes in the body and brain. Regular exercise reduces the amount of adrenal hormones your body releases in response to stress. Also, with exercise, your body releases greater amounts of endorphins, the powerful, pain-relieving, mood-elevating chemicals in the brain. Depressed people often lack these neurochemicals. Endorphins are natural pain killers and also help lift your mood. The runner's high is a result of the increased endorphins in the body. Exercise, therefore, will keep your body functioning properly and will keep you feeling both relaxed, refreshed and promote deep, restful sleep.

Exercise seems to be a popular 'fix' for stress, this is something that must be approached with caution. For people who have a sedentary job or lifestyle it could work wonders. For the person who is already overworked and physically drained it simply does not make any sense whatsoever to add any additional workload.

Begin an exercise that you enjoy, preferably, do something that brings you into contact with other people. The value of such exercise, three times a week for 20 minutes to two hours, can not be over emphasised.

Problems always seem less important when you are walking, swimming, running, cycling, or are involved in any physical pursuit; apart from the mental benefits, physical exercise uses up excess adrenaline

Exercise has another beneficial effect. Most people, when exercising, do not worry. They are actually resting the nerve cells in the brain that worry, giving those cells time to renew themselves, so they can function normally the next time they are needed. There are other ways of "resting your mind". Dancing, listening to music, reading, working on a craft, playing a musical instrument, meditation, self relaxation, and biofeedback also relieve stress. Any activity which concentrates your attention on a subject other than life's problems will help rest your mind. This allows the brain to renew itself.

Aerobic vs. Anaerobic Exercise

There are two types of exercise that perform different functions. Aerobic exercise is sustained activity involving the major muscle groups, such as swimming, running, or brisk walking. Your heart and respiratory rate increase, and more oxygen is circulated through the body. This kind of exercise strengthens your cardiovascular system and increases your overall strength and stamina. The goal of aerobic exercise is for your pulse to reach a training rate that is appropriate for your age. You must stay at the rate for twenty minutes, and exercise three times a week, in order to reap the benefits of aerobic exercise.

You've probably heard of "low-impact," or anaerobic, exercise. This means that you are not exercising vigorously or long enough to reach and maintain your training heart rate. It does not mean, however, that low-impact exercise is useless. It improves your muscle strength and flexibility and can still be a good outlet for negative feelings that you might have bottled up.

There are three kinds of anaerobic exercise.

Isotonics require that your muscles contract against a resistant object with movement, such as in weight lifting. Isometric exercises increase strength without building bulk.

Calisthenics are stretching exercises, such as sit-ups, toe-touches, and knee-bends, help increase flexibility and joint mobility.

The kinds of exercises you choose to do depend on your physical ability as well as your preferences. The most important rule is to choose activities that you enjoy and that are accessible and feasible for you to do regularly. You also should consider whether you want to make your exercise routine personal time in which you can be alone with your thoughts or a more as a social activity. Some people find that exercising with others provides them with support and encouragement and it can even be fun!

Before you begin an exercise programme, you should have a physical examination. If you are over the age of forty, your doctor will probably want to do a stress electrocardiogram to determine how much activity your heart can handle. If you have not exercised regularly for some time, begin slowly with low-impact exercise and gradually increase your activity. If you experience any adverse side effects, such as dizziness, cramps, or chest pain, stop exercising and consult your physician.

A Good Exercise Programme

There are a number of aspects to a good exercise programme.

Regular Physical Work

This should be endurance-type work – i.e., effort that is sustainable for at least 20 to 60 minutes.

This work should be primarily aerobic with intermittent bouts of anaerobic work.

Exercise should be done at least five days consecutively, each week.

The human body craves consistency and can make adjustments to long-term demands placed upon it. If you exercise three times per week, it will have a conditioning effect on your heart, but the heart is not the only thing that needs to perform efficiently during exercise. The other organs and muscle tissues will respond much differently to five days in a row. For five days in a row, the body continues to receive the message that it needs to perform efficiently in order to keep up. It adjusts to meet the demand and the result is efficient operation of the whole system, all the time, even on the two days you don't exercise.

Most people gain weight due to stress and not because of increased food intake or reduction in activity levels. Combining regular, vigorous exercise along with eliminating stress can bring about a reversal: significant weight reduction.

Five days of regular, vigorous exercise does stimulate efficiency throughout the body. Too much vigorous exercise can cause the body to go into the survival mode and cause damage to the regular efficient system. This is why it is vital that exercise is begun gradually and increased gradually.

Low Impact Exercise for Home

Following is a basic low-impact exercise routine that you can do at home. Remember that this does not provide aerobic workout-for that you must choose an activity such as bicycling, running, brisk walking, swimming, aerobic dance, or use a machine such as a stationary bicycle, Lifecycle, Stairmaster, or treadmill. When you exercise, wear loose, comfortable clothing and supportive sneakers. Wait two hours after a meal before exercising in order to avoid cramping or nausea, and be sure to drink plenty of water before, during, and after your workout.

Warming Up (at least five minutes)

Stand with your feet a shoulder-width apart, your arms at your sides. Gently roll your head in a half circle in front of you, back and forth a few times. With your head straight, drop your left ear to your shoulder and hold. Bring your head to centre and drop your right ear to your shoulder and hold. Bring your head back up and drop your chin to your chest. Head up and drop it back. Bring your head back up and face forward.

Shrug your shoulders up and release; repeat this six times. Roll your shoulders backward six times; roll them forward six times.

Place your left hand on your hip and raise your right arm up. Keeping your torso straight, reach your right arm over your head, bending to the left from your waist. Hold and then return to centre. Repeat with the left arm reaching over your head to the right. You should feel a stretch in your sides.

Stand with your feet slightly more than a shoulder- width apart. Reach down your left leg as far as you can, trying to touch your ankle or toes if possible. Hold for ten seconds. Slowly roll yourself upright, keeping your head down to avoid dizziness. Now reach down your right leg in the same manner and hold. Again, roll up slowly with your head down. This stretches the muscles in the backs of your legs.

Still standing with your feet apart, turn to your left. Bend your left knee and extend your right leg straight out behind you. Centre your body so that your left knee is bent at a 90-degree angle to the floor. Hold this position, called a runner's stretch, for a count of ten, gently pressing your straight leg down toward the floor. You'll feel the stretch in the thigh muscle of the out-stretched leg. Repeat this exercise with your right leg.

To stretch your Achilles tendon and calf muscles, stand two to three feet from a wall and place your hands on it. Keeping your legs straight and your feet flat on the floor, lean in to the wall. You should feel the stretch in your legs; hold it for ten seconds. Try stepping back a bit farther to increase the stretch; remember that your feet should remain flat on the floor.

Exercising and Conditioning (15-20 minutes)

With all of the following exercises, be sure to do the repetitions slowly and evenly, with some tension in your limbs. Your arms should not simply swing back and forth, but should move in a controlled, deliberate way, almost as if they were resisting against an invisible weight.

All of these suggest ten repetitions, but if you are just starting out, do as many as you feel comfortable doing. "No pain, no gain" may be true to some extent for accomplished athletes, but for the average person, pain often signifies stress. Try to stay tuned to the sensations in your muscles and use common sense. If it hurts too much, it's time to stop. As you exercise, your muscle tissue actually breaks down. In order to allow your muscles time to restore themselves, work out every other day or exercise various body areas on alternating days.

Arms

Stand with your feet a shoulder-width apart, stomach tucked in, and back straight. Extend your arms out to the sides with you, palms facing out. Bring your arms in together straight out in front of you, palms out, and extend back out. Do ten repetitions.

2. Keeping your arms extended, bring them straight up together above your head, then drop them so that they extend out to the sides. Repeat ten times.

3. Arms still extended with palms facing out, move your arms forward in small circles. Do ten of these and then increase to a medium-size circle. Do ten repetitions and then ten more, making the largest circle you can. Repeat this cycle, moving your arms backward.

4. Extend your arms out to the sides, bend them at the elbows, and make fists. Squeeze your bent arms together so that your forearms meet in front of you. This exercise works the chest and arms.

5. To work your biceps, extend your arms straight down at your sides with your inner forearms and fists facing up. Bending at the elbow, squeeze your fists to your shoulders. In order to obtain the maximum benefit, pretend that there is a weight on your inner forearm and resist against the pressure as you squeeze up.

Waist

Standing with your feet a shoulder-width apart, bend to the left, reaching slightly down and out as far as you can with your left arm. Your right hand can remain on your hip or your elbow can raise up simultaneously as you are reaching to the side with your left arm. Do ten repetitions and then repeat with the right side.

Standing with your feet apart, place your hands on your hips or raise your arms to chest level and bend them at the elbows so that your forearms are directly in front of your chest. Keeping your hips straight, move from the waist, twisting ten times to the left and ten times to the right. Then try alternating, pausing in the forward position between each twist.

This one may be a little harder to do. Sit on the floor with your legs spread open as wide as possible and your hands clasped behind your head. Keeping your back straight and your elbows back, reach down toward the floor behind your left knee with your left elbow. Come up, pause, and then reach down toward the floor with your right elbow. Do ten repetitions.

Abdomen

Sit on the floor with your knees slightly bent and your back straight. You can hold your arms straight out in front of you for balance, or you can cross them over your chest. From this sitting position, slowly roll back so that your shoulders are just a few inches above the floor. Pause and then slowly roll back up to a sitting position. As you do this exercise, always press the small of your back downward, rather than arching your back, in order to prevent strain. Do ten repetitions.

Lie on the floor with your stomach tucked in so that the small of your back presses down toward the floor. Bend your knees slightly and keep your feet flat on the floor. Clasp your hands behind your head, and, keeping your elbows back as much as possible, slowly raise your head and shoulders up off the ground. In order to help you do this exercise properly, pick a spot on the ceiling and raise your chin up toward that spot. Your head, neck, and shoulders should stay aligned and straight; you should not be "hunching" up, tucking your chin in, or using your elbows and arms to pull you up. If you don't do this exercise in the proper way, your abdomen will not benefit at all. If you do it properly, however, you will feel your abdominal muscles contract as you come up and relax as you come down. Do ten repetitions slowly and rhythmically.

This is a more advanced form of exercise 2. Lying in the same position, rest your left leg on your right knee. Lift your head and shoulders up in the same manner as above. Do ten repetitions and then switch legs for ten more.

Thighs

Sit on the floor with your back straight, your hands on the floor to your sides and slightly behind you with your arms straight to support your body. Keeping your right leg relaxed, straighten your left leg, point your toe, and slowly raise it up about a foot off the ground. Lower the leg and repeat ten times. Switch legs and repeat ten times with your right leg. Remember to keep your back straight as you do this exercise.

Inner Thighs

Sitting in the same position as in the "Thighs" exercise with your legs extended straight out in front of you, lift your left leg a few inches off the floor, point your toe, and slowly move it out to the left. You'll feel a nice stretch on the inside of your thigh. Bring your leg back to the starting position, and repeat ten times. Switch legs and repeat ten times with your right leg.

Outer Thighs

Lie on your left side, your left arm bent at the elbow so that your hand supports your head, your legs stacked on top of each other. Make sure that your back is straight, and tilt your pelvis slightly toward the floor. Bend your bottom leg at the knee and keep this leg relaxed. Straighten your top leg, toe pointed, and raise it up as far as you can. You want to keep your leg straight as you raise it so that the outer thigh is parallel with the ceiling. Lower your leg and repeat ten times. When you do this exercise, pretend that there is a weight on your outer thigh and resist against it as you raise your leg. This will maximise the benefit to your muscles. Do ten repetitions and then lie on your opposite side and work your opposite leg.

Buttocks

Lie on your back, your knees bent with your feet apart, your hands clasped behind your head or placed under your buttocks. Without arching your back, lift your buttocks off the floor. Squeeze your buttocks with each lift and then release as you come back to the floor. Do ten repetitions with your feet apart and then ten with your feet together. As you master this exercise, you can do it keeping your feet apart with your knees together; with your feet together and your knees spread apart. Those who are more advanced can cross one leg over the opposite knee and vice versa.

Using the stretches described in the warm-up, be sure to spend at least five minutes cooling down after your exercise routine. If you do aerobic exercise, cool down by slowing your pace for five minutes as well as doing five minutes of stretching exercises. For example, when you're done jogging or bicycling, take a brisk walk to cool down; if you swim, cool down by doing gentle breast-, back-, or sidestrokes for five minutes. Although you may be tempted sometimes to skip the stretching, remember that your muscles have contracted and tightened during exercise, and they must be stretched out in order to prevent cramping and injuries, such as pulls.

Some Recommendations for Improved Fitness

Do Aerobic exercises such as those mentioned below regularly

- Walking in the woods, at the beach, or in a park

- Participating in a sporting event, such as tennis, basketball, volleyball, racquetball, softball, and many others.
- Riding a bicycle.
- Practicing yoga.
- Practicing some form of martial art such as karate, taikwando, kung fu, tai chi and so on.

You can do yogic exercises in order to stretch your muscles, activate them and relax later on through techniques suggested in yogic practices. We will, in the next chapter cover the physical and spiritual dimensions of yoga in a more descriptive way, more from a spiritual perspective than physical and mental. However, it is enough to say now that yoga as a form of a set of exercises practiced for the benefits of health will prepare your body and mind ready for a journey of spirituality and enlightenment, the concepts of which the author wishes to share with the reader in the next chapter.

An Exercise for the Neck

When you are stressed, often the first place you feel it is your neck. Try this four-way neck release recommended by former world-class track and field athlete Greg Herzog in his book, *"The 15 Minute Executive Stress Relief Program"* (repeat each of the following exercises three times):

With your right hand, reach over your head and behind your left ear, grasping your neck with your fingers. Pull your head gently toward your right shoulder.

Do the same exercise, but this time use your left hand to pull your head toward your left shoulder.

Clasp your hands behind your head, with your elbows flared and your head bowed toward your chest. Relax in this position for 30 seconds. Then while pulling down with your hands, slowly push your head back until you are looking at the ceiling.

Place the palm of your left hand on your forehead, with the bottom of your palm at the bridge of your nose. Hold your right arm across your body so that you can rest your left elbow on your right wrist. Now push against your left palm with your forehead while keeping your right arm locked. Switch hands and repeat.

Deep Breathing

Deep breathing infuses the blood with extra oxygen and also stimulates the body to release tranquilizing endorphins. It is one of the simplest yet most effective stress management techniques. You can do it anywhere, anytime, and it becomes even more effective with practice.

Nature Walks and Imagery

We know the feeling when we sit in the beach and see the sun set or sit on the brink of grand canyon looking at the view. We are so much into appreciating the beauty and the awe of the god's creation, we forget about our other problems. It is like meditation. We are transported to a different world. This is a great way to get rid of stress from our system. Take frequent nature walks. Watch the magnificent sunset. Listen to good music and let it transport you to distant realms. Stop and smell the rose and marvel at its beauty. All of these that pleases the senses calms the mind as well. So give yourself time-and opportunity-to indulge your senses. Let your little pleasures bring relief from big problems!

Nature is one of the best soothers of stress. Taking a quiet walk in a park or watching a beautiful sunset can do wonders. Even reminiscing about such a scene from your past, or simply imagining one, allows your stress level to drop. Picture a trip to a palm-studded beach in Hawaii, whether you've been there or not. Or imagine a lush waterfall in Vanuatu. Or a trip to Malabar Coast!

Hydrotherapy: A Warm, Hot Bath

Hot baths can do more than keep you clean. It has been found that warm baths (water temperature between 100 to 102 degree F) not only relax the muscles but help provide some quiet time as well. So when you need to escape, fill the tub, lie back, and relax.

Generally, heat quiets and soothes the body, slowing down the activity of internal organs. Cold, in contrast, stimulates and invigorates, increasing internal activity. If you are experiencing tense muscles and anxiety from your stress, a hot shower or bath is in order. If you are feeling tired and stressed out, you might want to try taking a warm shower or bath followed by a short, invigorating cold shower to help stimulate your body and mind. Experiment with different water temperatures and durations in the bath or shower to determine what water method works best for you. Remember, the goal is to use hydrotherapy to achieve a state of comfort, relaxation, and refreshment.

Water seems to have special powers in getting rid of stress and rejuvenating our body. It affects the skin and muscles. It calms the lungs, heart, stomach, and endocrine system by stimulating nerve reflexes on the spinal cord.

When you submerge yourself in a bath, a pool, or a whirlpool, you experience a kind of weightlessness. Your body is relieved from the constant pull of gravity. Water also has a hydrostatic effect. It has a massage-like feeling as the water gently kneads your body. Water, in motion, stimulates touch receptors on the skin, boosting blood circulation and releasing tight muscles.

The more the water is in motion, higher is its stress-relieving benefits. In a study of 40 persons at University of Minnesota, 85 per cent of the participants preferred a whirlpool bath to a still bath. Only whirlpool was effective in reducing the participants' reactivity to stress although both still and whirlpool baths were effective in reducing anxiety.

Herbal baths can be particularly soothing when you are experiencing a period of stress.

Music Therapy

Listening to music does wonders to alleviate stress. Please note that everyone has different tastes in music. Listen to the music that you feel comfortable. Sitting down and forcing yourself to listen to relaxation music that you don't like may create stress, not alleviate it.

Music has always been a great healer. In the Bible, we learn about how David played the harp to help ease his severe depression of King Saul.

Music is a significant mood-changer and reliever of stress, working on many levels at once.

Many experts suggest that it is the rhythm of the music or the beat that has the calming effect on us although we may not be very conscious about it. They point out that when we were a baby in our mother's womb, we probably were influenced by the heartbeat of our mother. We respond to the soothing music at later stages in life, perhaps associating it with the safe, relaxing, protective environment provided by our mother.

Music can be one of the most soothing or nerve-wracking experiences available. Choosing what will work for any individual is difficult, most will choose something they 'like' instead of what might be beneficial. In doing extensive research on what any given piece of music produces in the physiological response system many unexpected things were found. Many of the so-called Meditation and Relaxation recordings actually produced adverse EEG patterns, just as bad as Hard Rock and Heavy Metal. The surprising thing was many selections of Celtic, Native American as well as various music containing loud drums or flute were extremely soothing. The most profound finding was any music Performed Live and even at moderately loud volumes even if it was somewhat discordant had very a beneficial response. Whenever the proper sounds were experienced an amazing right and left brain hemisphere synchronisation occurred. The normal voltage spiking pattern changed to a smooth sinusoidal waveform and the usual voltage differential equalised. The entire human energetic system is extremely influenced by sounds, the physical body and chakra centres respond specifically to certain tones and frequencies. Special consideration should be given to the positive effects of one actually playing or creating music themselves.

Among the first stress-fighting changes that take place when we hear a tune is an increase in deep breathing. The body's production of serotonin also accelerates.

Music was found to reduce the pain during dental procedures.

Playing music in the background while we are working, seemingly unaware of the music itself, has been found to reduce the stress.

Music was found to reduce heart rates and to promote higher body temperature - an indication of the onset of relaxation. Combining music with relaxation therapy was more effective than doing relaxation therapy alone.

Maximising With Music Therapy

As we mentioned before, there is not a single music that is good for everyone. People have different tastes. It is important that you like the music being played.

Introduction to Sleep Disorders

Sound, restorative sleep is the foundation of a healthy life. A good night's sleep is undoubtedly one of the most precious gifts we can enjoy.

Sleep provides the rest our body needs. Rest is the basis of activity. If you sleep well at night, you function well in the daytime. If you don't sleep well, you don't function up to par. Your reactions are slower, your mind feels heavy and dull, you tend to get upset more easily, you don't work as efficiently, and, in general, it's a lot harder to get through the day. Thus, sleep is vital for healthy brain activity during the day. A wholesome sleep ensures that your moods, emotions, reflexes, and cognitive ability are at their best when you are awake.

Happiness and misery, obesity and leanness, strength and weakness, sexual vigour and impotence, consciousness and loss of sensory acuity, even life and death, depend on the quality of sleep.

In spite of the fact that importance of good sleep had been known well before Christ's birth, sleep complaints are very common today. Several studies have clearly shown that sleep complaints are very common in the general population. One study conducted over a two-year period (1978 to 1980), included 4698 patients, each of whom underwent a polysomnographic (PSG) study. The proportions of diagnostic categories in those with sleep complaints, after those evaluated for impotency are excluded were:

51 per cent with hypersomnia

31 per cent with insomnia

15 per cent with parasomnia

3 per cent with sleep-wake schedule disorders.

A subsequent study on 3085 patients over a one-year period (1981 to 1982) showed remarkable consistency with the results of the first study. The most frequent disease categories included in these surveys were sleep apnea, narcolepsy, and insomnia related to psychiatric or psychophysiologic disorders. A study by The Institute of Medicine in 1979 concluded that about one-third of all adults in USA had some sleep disturbances. Risk factors for sleep complaints identified were:

Old age

Female sex

Poor education and socio-economic status

Recent stress

Alcohol and drug abuse

Despite this high prevalence of sleep disturbances, most of the patients who visit a primary care physician with sleep complaints will not be properly diagnosed. William C. Dement. MD estimated that family practitioners catch fewer than one or two per cent of their patients with apnea. Even those with the most flagrant symptoms are rarely identified.

Missing sleep is more than inconvenient. Recurrent insomnia can throw the whole system out of balance and can lead to chronic fatigue. Researchers have made an association between insomnia and other diseases, such as depression and anxiety. It robs you from enjoying good relationships with friends and family members.

It's very important that we do whatever we need to do in order to sleep well. Addressing sleep disorders is a very important step you can take to have a healthy, wholesome life. Good sleep is foundation for increased stamina, resistance to disease, slower aging process, and elevated mood.

The most common form of sleep disorder is insomnia-the inability to fall asleep and stay asleep throughout the night. Other common sleep complaints are: Snoring, Sleep Apnea, Narcolepsy, Restless leg syndrome, Sleepwalking, Night Terrors, Nightmares, Bedwetting, etc. However, these are only a very small fraction of the disorders listed in the International Classification of Sleep Disorders by American Sleep Disorders Association.

The consequences of inadequate sleep can be dangerous. Healthy men deprived of even a single night's sleep have a 30 per cent drop in the activity of their immune system's tumor-fighting cells the next day. The electrical activity in the brain during dream sleep puts a stop to muscle activity. This allows the body to reconstruct damaged muscle tissue. Lack of sleep means that your body does not get enough time it needs to repair worn-out tissue. People who had inadequate sleep in a night was found to experience a surge of high blood pressure when they wake up in the morning. In some cases, that surge can lead to stroke or other heart problems.

Sleep problems add several billion dollars to the nation's total costs for healthcare each year.

According to the U.S. Department of Transportation, each year two hundred thousand sleep-related accidents claim more than five thousand lives (some put the number at closer to twenty-three thousand deaths). Sleepy drivers also cause accidents that results in hundreds of thousands of injuries and a large number of deaths. In a survey of physicians, 42 per cent of them admitted that they had caused the death of at least one person because they had been too sleepy to make wise medical decisions or perform surgery properly.

How much sleep you need in a day? It depends on the individuals. Many people can get by on five or six hours a night. Others need nine or ten hours.

Sleep needs generally decrease with age. A one-year-old baby requires about fourteen hours of sleep a day. By age five, children need about twelve hours. Adults, on an average, need about seven to eight hours. Women tend to require more sleep than men. Many elderly people sleep less than their younger counterparts. They tend to sleep less at night but doze more during the day than younger adults.

Chapter - 9

Spirituality in Life Yoga, Meditation, Prayer, Freedom and Enlightenment The Ultimate Concepts Related to Stress-free Living

"You do not see anything when you experience pure consciousness; you become everything." —*Sebastian Pole*

A Brief Philosophy of Yoga (Ref 1, 3, 4)

The yogis consider that we are all searching for happiness and that this is everybody's main goal. It's just that most people settle for the brief, watered-down version of temporary pleasures.

The yogis state that at some stage in our spiritual evolution over many lives we will become dissatisfied with brief, temporary pleasures and start our quest for eternal bliss. Methods to achieve this were developed and perfected by the yogis thousands of years ago. They consider that nature's laws are so designed that we must evolve. The main mechanism nature uses in the early stages is pain. When we find that relationships, money or alcohol, for example, do not produce happiness or a sense of purpose, we will start looking more deeply into life. Yoga waits patiently for you to reach this stage.

In the later stages of spiritual evolution, pain is no longer needed to spur us on. Each stage of progress produces such peace and happiness that this entices us to go to a higher level of happiness. Thus, instead of pain, reward of happiness becomes the prime mover.

The above is a very brief indication of yoga philosophy, which is so comprehensive that it deals with every aspect of life and delves into the very nature of reality. It is obviously beyond the scope of this book.

What is Yoga?

In practice, yoga is an applied science of the mind and body. It comes from the Hindu vedas (scriptures). Practice and study of it help to bring about a natural balance of body and mind in which the state of health can manifest itself. Yoga itself does not create health; rather, it creates an internal environment that allows the individual to come to his own state of dynamic balance, or health. Basically, yoga teaches that a healthy person is a harmoniously integrated unit of body, mind and spirit. Therefore, good health requires a simple, natural diet, exercise in fresh air, a serene and untroubled mind and the awareness that main's deepest and highest self is identical with the spirit of God. As a result, to many devotees, yoga becomes a philosophy that offers instruction and insight into every aspect of life: the spiritual, the mental and the physical. Of course, because it is all-encompassing, people who want to pick and choose from its smorgasbord can do so without being disappointed. Yoga is equally satisfying as a physical therapy alone.

The Yoga System

One basic assumption of the Yoga Sutras is that the body and the mind are part of one continuum of existence, the mind being more subtle than the body. This is the foundation of the yogic view of health. The interaction of body and mind is the central concern of the entire science. It is believed that as the body and mind are brought into balance and health, the individual will be able to perceive his true nature; this will allow life to be lived through him more freely and spontaneously.

Yoga first attempts to reach the mind, where health begins, for mental choices strongly affect the health of the body. Choices of food, types of exercise, which thoughts to think, etc. all affect the body. As practiced traditionally in India, yoga includes a set of ethical imperatives and moral precepts, including diet, exercise, and meditative aspects. In the West, yoga focuses primarily on postures (gentle stretching exercises), breathing exercises, and meditation.

Yoga is frequently used in Western medicine to enhance health and treat chronic disease as well as stress.

Yoga therapy begins with relaxation. Living in an age of anxiety, we are often unconscious of our tensions. We are often depressed, tired, and an easy victim of diseases. There are a number of reasons for our stressful life. Often it is lack of rest, anxiety, tension and fatigue. These are constantly draining our health energies continuously. Thus, the first priority is to get us into a relaxed state. Yoga employs asanas, pranayama (breathing exercises) and meditation and/or visualisation.

Asanas (postures)

Postures are gentle stretching movements designed to help balance the mind and body. The yoga postures are designed to rejuvenate the brain, spine, glands and internal organs. They work by increasing the blood and prana supply to these areas and by stimulating them with a gentle squeezing action

The asanas were designed with economy of time and effort in mind. Most of them work on more than one aspect of the body at the same time. For example, the twist asana benefits the spine, adrenal glands, liver, pancreas and kidneys.

The yoga asanas produce their beneficial effect on the organs and glands in three ways:

- The position of the asana causes an increase in blood circulation to the specific target organ or gland.
- The position of the asana often produces a slight squeezing of the organ or gland. This has the effect of massaging the organ or gland and stimulating it.
- Deep breathing and visualizing the target area sends an extra supply of prana to the area.

Yoga's effect on the spine is to increase its flexibility. This ensures a good nerve supply to all parts of the body, since the nerves from the spine go to all the organs and glands.

Pranayama as Part of Ashtanga Yoga

Concentration/Meditation practices: The benefits of the postures are greater if you concentrate the healing action where it is needed. You can incorporate a variety of affirmations, meditation/ concentration practices and visualisation. Meditation and concentration is covered in detail elsewhere. Many times focusing on an object or sound (like clicking of a clock) can help us concentrate and leave our distracting thoughts away.

An affirmation is a declaratory statement of yourself. They are inner-self conditioners. Our inner mind will believe everything we say with conviction and emotional force. It take some persistent repetitions to get the desired result. Typical affirmations that can be used are:

- I am at my desired weight (for dieters)
- My lungs are pure and clean (for smokers who want to get out of the habit)
- I feel continuously alert, vital and useful (general), etc.

Even more powerful technique than affirmation is visualisation. Here, we show our subconscious mind a picture of what we are talking about. Forming such picture inside your mind is called visualisation.

To be effective, visualisation should involve all senses, not just sight. Imagine the state or thing we want. How does it feel when we have it? What will you be with it? What does it feel? What does it look like? How does it sound? How does it taste? How does it smell? For healing therapy, visualize the state without the condition. For example, for those trying to lose weight, visualize yourself in the desired weight and physical condition and imagine the life in the new state.

In other words, you should mentally see the affected area as it receives fresh blood circulation, oxygen and physical massage. A diabetic should visualize the healing energies flowing into the pancreas, near the stomach. A rheumatic can concentrate on the release of synovial fluid. Synovial fluid is a lubricant and also disperses waste matter which can cause stiffness at joints.

Thus, most effective yoga therapy involves a three-pronged attack. When you practice yoga postures, you are strengthening the body. When you control your breathing, you are creating a chemical and emotional balance. And when you concentrate your mind on affirmations, you are practicing the power of prayer. But when all three approaches are synthesised, you are entering the most powerful mystery of healing: the basic harmony of life.

Yoga's View of Disease

Yoga considers that most diseases are due to insufficient life force, either in the body as a whole, or a blockage of life force to one part of the body. This leads to a lowered body resistance or immunity to disease.

Those practicing yoga have learned many centuries ago that most diseases are due to reduced immunity. Medical science is gradually coming to the same conclusion.

When the whole body has lowered life force, the result is a lowered vitality level, poor health and susceptibility to infection. No infections would occur if the body's life force is high enough to fight off the infection. Pathogens (bacteria, viruses and so on) are a normal part of life and will only cause trouble when the body's resistance is too low to keep them in check.

The best way to increase the general life force of the body is by good nutrition, sufficient deep steep, a positive mental attitude and yoga.

A blockage of life force to one part of the body, such as the thyroid gland, is usually caused by a slight misalignment of a vertebra which impinges on the nerve that travels to that particular organ. This causes an interference to the life force (nerve impulses) to the organ. As a result, the organ not functioning at its optimum level. If the spinal misalignment is not corrected, the organ may develop pathology. It is much more difficult to correct at this stage.

The ancient yogis were well aware of the importance of the spine in relation to disease, since most of their asanas or postures were designed to make the spine more flexible to prevent spinal misalignments. Some of the asanas will even correct minor spinal misalignments.

The spine is so important for a high vitality level, good health and the correction of many health conditions that a whole science of healing has been developed to correct spinal misalignments. In fact, chiropractic is now the second largest healing profession after medicine and the fastest growing healing profession in the world.

Types of Yoga

One of the features of yoga, which can be confusing at first, is that a variety of forms of yoga are practiced. Together, they are called yoga. While these share common elements, some focus more on postures and breathing exercises, whereas others have a greater focus on spirituality. Each emphasises a particular path that comprises a certain set of beliefs, practices, and rituals. Yoga forms constitute a ladder of sorts, from the "lowest" form of Hatha yoga, with its focus on physical postures and breathing techniques, to the "highest" form known as Raja, or "union by mental mastery."

Newer forms of hybrids of yoga are also proposed such as Power yoga or Acu-yoga. There are also variations of yoga depending on "the teacher that is being followed."

The most popular forms of yoga are:

- Hatha Yoga ("the yoga of vitality') - The Foundation
- Bhakti Yoga: The Yoga of Love
- Karma Yoga ("the yoga of action") - the Yoga of Selfless Action
- Jnana Yoga: The Yoga of Knowledge
- Raja Yoga- The Highest form of yoga
- Mantra Yoga
- Laya, Tantra or Kundalini Yoga
- Integral Yoga (Purna Yoga)

Hatha Yoga ("the yoga of vitality") -The Foundation

An easy-to-learn basic form of yoga. Very popular in India and even in the United States. Hatha Yoga is the foundation of all Yoga systems. Hatha Yoga is the preparation for higher Yogas. Ha means "sun" and tha means "moon." Thus, Hatha Yoga refers to positive (sun) and to negative (moon) currents in the system. These currents are to be balanced and mastered so that vital force, prana, can be regulated, the mind cleared and superconscious states experienced.

The ideal way to practice the Hatha Yoga poses (asanas) is to approach the practice session in a calm, meditative mood. Sit quietly for a few moments, then begin the series, slowly, with control and grace, being inwardly aware as the body performs the various poses selected for the practice session. Do not overdo the asanas or try to compete with others. Take it easy and enjoy.

Bhakti Yoga

Bhakti Yoga is the system in which love and devotion are emphasised. There are Bhakti Yoga traditions that do not teach asana, pranayama, mudra or controlled meditation - main practices of traditional yoga. Instead, love of God, love of God in man, and surrender to God's will is stressed in the Bhakti Yoga approach. Some people are naturally inclined by temperament to be devotional and to love God and God-as-the-world. Balance is recommended: devotion balanced with reason, love balanced with understanding.

There are no set ways to perform Bhakti yoga. Some people find that external aids can contribute to a devotional attitude: an altar used during prayer and meditation; pictures of saints to serve as inspiration; chanting or singing; use of mantra or even a simple devotional ceremony to aid in creating a mood as preparation for meditation. Whatever a person's approach, if that approach is useful in the long run, it is perfectly in order for him, even though it may not appeal to another.

Singing the names of God aloud can elevate consciousness, clear the mind and even charge the environment with pure energy. For persons who find it difficult to concentrate during meditation and for whom the approach of calm discernment is too subtle, prayer and chanting can be of value.

It is in our day to day life that Bhakti Yoga is truly practiced. Are we loving, compassionate and fair in our dealings with others? St. Francis is one of the Christian tradition who exemplified the Yoga of love and devotion. Jesus stated the ideal of Bhakti Yoga when he taught, "As you have loved me, love one another." When true love reigns, there can be no barriers; then harmony and fulfillment rule.

Simple, direct prayer is the most effective- just talking with God, then being still. The teaching is that by devotion and receptivity we can open ourselves to the Reality of God and attract God's consciousness into our own. Love and devotion also purifies human nature and cleanses the mind and the emotional field. There can be no hate, dislike, jealousy, envy, fear or prejudice in the loving heart.

Truly, blessed are the pure in heart, for they can perceive the Reality of God.

Karma Yoga ("the yoga of action") : the Yoga of Selfless Action

This yoga emphasises selfless action and service, such as that practiced by Mahatma Gandhi.

The message of Karma Yoga is this: when we work in harmony with the Power that runs the universe, we are not egotistically motivated, and we no longer maintain compulsive desires relative to the future. With the eradication of compulsive desire, we are able to live in the present, while planning for the future, without being bound to the future. Every reasonable desire carries within itself the motive force for its fulfillment. That is, if an experience is possible to have in this natural world, and we desire it, we are subconsciously pushed toward it or attract it to ourselves.

Yogic philosophy does not ask us to give up intelligent planning. It says to renounce egotistic desire. We are then able to be open to inner guidance and to flow in the stream of grace. The Intelligence-Power that sustains the universe has a plan and a purpose. When we are in harmony with it we are free, even while involved.

As we work with a cheerful attitude, doing what we are best suited to do, we know a harmony and an inner peace which those who strive and struggle can never know.

Raja Yoga- The Highest Form of Yoga (Ref 1)

Raja means "royal," and the meditation route to Self-Realisation is considered to be just this. It is direct and affords the opportunity of experience in different levels of awareness, beginning from where we start to where we are able to conclude after our meditation practice. Raja Yoga starts with the mind; its goal is a complete stilling of the mind, so that the light of the indwelling spirit may shine out. It makes use of asana and pranayama, and some consider it merely another name for Ashtanga Yoga, described elsewhere.

Raja Yoga meditation is the process whereby the practitioner concentrates upon one point in order to integrate discontinuous, diffused attention, thus holding attention steady. All distractions are thus effectively closed out, and meditation proceeds. Day-dreaming, floating with thoughts or allowing impulses to dominate is obviously not concentration, and, without concentration, meditation is impossible to experience.

Mantra Yoga

Mantra yoga means "union by voice or sound". This form includes the rhythmic repetitions of specific sounds, chants, or mantras. The practitioner repeats the syllable, word or phrase continually, sometimes for weeks, months or years on end. Certain syllables are believed to posses healing potential for specific purposes. (for example, see Transcendental meditation where a mantra is assigned for individual use.)

Laya, Tantra or Kundalini Yoga

A celibate approach to spiritual growth is quite common in many of the world's religious traditions. Many yoga practices suggest that sexual involvement is a detriment to a greater development of self and hence should be avoided if possible. However, tantric yoga suggests that sexuality can be a very powerful force that can be harnessed for increased self-awareness. Thus, tantric yoga is unusual, in that it not only allows sexual feelings and contact, but usės sexual experience as a means to enlightenment.

The Tantrics maintain that there is an enormous energy locked into sexuality, which, if released from the lower end of the spine, can flow up the spinal column to bring divine illumination to the brain. They believe that within the interior of the spine, in a hollow region called the canalis. In centralis, there is an energy conduit called "sushumna". Along this conduit, from the base of the perineum to the top of the head, flows the most powerful of all psychic energies, Kundalini energy. On the other side of the canal are two additional energy channels, one called "Ida" corresponding to the male, and the other the "Pingala" corresponding to the female. Ida is at the right of the base of the spine and the pingala begins at the left.

These two psychic currents are said to coil upward around the spine and the sushumna like snakes, crossing the chakras (energy wheel of centre of conscious). Kundalini yogi's lifelong task is to evolve through the various chakra qualities and challenges, thereby bringing the focus of the Kundalini energy upward from the base of his spine to the top of his head.

Once the yogi has achieved mastery of self by relaxing body tension, silencing mental chatter, and releasing energy blocks, he is ready to join with a partner whose energies and spirit complement his own in such a way that together they form a "whole". The partners must first achieve a highly developed awareness within their being, a process that might take a lifetime, before ready to engage in tantric embrace. In the tantric love-making experience, known as "maithuna", the lovers undergo a variety of meditations and rituals before they actually make physical contact. They maintain the spiritual link or bond throughout the love-making process. They visualise the flow of pranic currents between them. In tantric yoga, the lovers do not try to achieve orgasm. In fact, they work hard not to have one. They are attempting to draw the forces of Kundalini energy upward through their body-minds, thus releasing the power of the various chakras. This force transforms the yogi psychologically, changing his personality as the Kundalini rises to each succeeding chakra. The emphasis is not on the sexual release as an end in and of itself, but rather on sex as a channel through which the evolution of self may proceed.

The goal of Tantra is the union of dynamic and static aspects of personality. It is quite different from practices that dwell on renunciation and desirelessness.

Integral (Purna) Yoga

Integral yoga is a modern version of the traditional yoga systems of India. Many contemporary philosophers felt that traditional yoga gives too much importance to the attainment of the salvation and too much emphasis to the next life that the present life is neglected. This yoga teaches that what you do every day (karma) is important Although traditional yoga always had karma or yoga of work as part of the arsenal all the time. It is the emphasis or importance on attaining the consciousness, outside space-time that is of issue here. Integral yoga gives yoga an affirmative and dynamic form. It places the spiritual ideal of life on the foundation of an integrated world-view that takes into account the evolutionary and historical perspective of life.

Integral yoga evokes three levels of integration: the integration of the inner environment or harmonisation of the human personality, the integration of the human psyche with its external environment, and the integration of the psyche with its ultimate spiritual Ground, or the Divine. It is a world-affirmative and body-positive spirituality that skillfully combines self-transcendence with love, compassion, and reverence for all life.

For integral yoga the ultimate goal of life is complete self-integration. Action, love, wisdom and peace are equally important elements in such self-integration. The yoga of love or devotion (Bhakti yoga) is perfectly right in affirming love as the fulfillment of life and as an essential ingredient of salvation. But integral yoga points out that love is inseparable from wisdom and selfless action. Love in its spiritual essence is an attribute of wisdom. It is active interest in the progress and betterment of society. Love is undivided loyalty to life's higher values.

The yoga of knowledge (Jnana yoga) is perfectly right in affirming knowledge as the fulfillment of life and an essential ingredient of salvation. But integral yoga points out that knowledge is inseparable from love and action. Knowledge in its essence is comprehensive awareness of the nature of existence.

The yoga of action (Karma yoga) is perfectly right in affirming action as the essence of human reality and as an essential condition of salvation. But integral yoga points out that action is not merely a means to self-purification resulting in salvation.

An unbridgeable gulf is believed to exist between nature and spirit, between body and soul. All forms of self-torture and mortification of the flesh are invented in order to help in the triumph of the spirit. According to integral yoga, freedom is not emancipation from Nature, but emancipation in Nature. The balanced growth of personality, complete self-integration or integral self-realisation, is the ideal for those practicing this yoga.

According to integral yoga, the values designated spiritual are no less an essential part of the spirit of Nature than the values designated material. The spirit may be defined as the higher mode of fulfillment of the creativity of Nature. And Nature may be regarded as the self-expressive energy and evolutionary dynamism of the spirit. So, both nature and spirit are equally important.

The dualism of matter and mind, nature and spirit, is inherent in the same evolutionary flux. Spiritual values emerge naturally and dualistically out of the organised and intelligent fulfillment of material values. When man intelligently co-operates with Nature, he gets rewarded with the treasures of the spirit. Integration of personality lays the foundation for an integrated outlook on life.

In integral self-realisation, the growth of personality is as important as the vision of the super-personal. It implies organised fulfillment of normal human desires. The growth of personality brings power and love. It represents a vision of new values and the hidden possibilities of life. Integral yoga aims at the unity of personality growth and spiritual intuition. It affirms the ideal of integrated personality as a creative centre of expression of the external.

There are three essential ingredients in the realisation of complete self-integration: psychic integration, cosmic integration, and existential integration. Integral yoga is the art of harmonious and creative living on the basis of the integral experience of Being. It aims at opening the springs of creative inspiration hidden in the human psyche. It aims at that serenity of self-poise which preserves the light of the eternal amidst the storm and stress of social living.

What is Meditation?

There are various types of meditation. Prayer is probably the best known, but there is also TM (Transcendental Meditation), mindfulness meditation, and from the Eastern tradition, Zen meditation, Buddhist meditation, and Taoist meditation.

Meditation Encompasses such Diverse Methods as Indicated below

Formal sitting in which the body is held immobile and the attention controlled. e.g., Zazen, Vipassana.

Expressive practices in which the body is let free and anything can happen. e.g., Siddha Yoga, the Latihan, the chaotic meditation of Rajneesh.

The practice of going about one's daily round of activities mindfully. e.g., Mahamudra, Shikan Taza, Gurdjieff's "self-remembering".

All these practices have one thing in common - They all focus on quietening the busy mind. The intention is not to remove stimulation but rather to direct your concentration to one healing element - one sound, one word, one image, or one's breath. When the mind is "filled" with the feeling of calm and peace, it cannot take off on its own and worry, stress out, or get depressed.

According to Joan Borysenko, Ph.D., a pioneer in the field of mind/body medicine, meditation can be broadly defined as any activity that keeps the attention pleasantly anchored in the present moment. When the mind is calm and focused in the present, it is neither reacting to memories from the past nor being preoccupied with plans for the future, two major sources of chronic stress known to impact health. "Meditation," says Dr Borysenko, "helps to keep us from identifying with the 'movies of the mind'."

Types of Meditation – Classification (Ref 1)

All the meditation techniques can be grouped into two basic approaches:

- Concentrative Meditation
- Mindfulness Meditation (Awareness Meditation)

Concentrative Meditation

Concentrative meditation focuses the attention on the breath, an image, or a sound (mantra), in order to still the mind and allow a greater awareness and clarity to emerge. This is like a zoom lens in a camera; we narrow our focus to a selected field.

The simplest form of concentrative meditation is to sit quietly and focus the attention on the breath. Yoga and meditation practitioners believe that there is a direct correlation between one's breath and one's state of the mind. For example, when a person is anxious, frightened, agitated, or distracted, the breath will tend to be shallow, rapid, and uneven. On the other hand, when the mind is calm, focused, and composed, the breath will tend to be slow, deep, and regular. Focusing the mind on the continuous rhythm of inhalation and exhalation provides a natural object of meditation. As you focus your awareness on the breath, your mind becomes absorbed in the rhythm of inhalation and exhalation. As a result, your breathing will become slower and deeper, and the mind becomes more tranquil and aware.

Mindfulness Meditation

Mindfulness meditation, according to Dr Borysenko, "involves opening the attention to become aware of the continuously passing parade of sensations and feelings, images, thoughts, sounds, smells, and so forth without becoming involved in thinking about them." The person sits quietly and simply witnesses whatever goes through the mind, not reacting or becoming involved with thoughts, memories, worries, or images. This helps to gain a more calm, clear, and non-reactive state of mind. Mindfulness meditation can be likened to a wide-angle lens. Instead of narrowing your sight to a selected field as in concentrative meditation, here you will be aware of the entire field.

How Meditation Works (Ref 1)

Studies have shown that meditation (in particular, research on Transcendental Meditation, a popular form of meditation practiced in the West for the past thirty years), can bring about a healthy state of relaxation by causing a generalised reduction in multiple physiological and biochemical markers, such as decreased heart rate, decreased respiration rate, decreased plasma cortisol (a major stress hormone), decreased pulse rate, and increased EEG (electroencephalogram) alpha, a brain wave associated with relaxation. Research done by R. Keith Wallace at U.C.L.A. on Transcendental Meditation, revealed that during meditation, the body gains a state of profound rest. At the same time, the brain and mind become more alert, indicating a state of restful alertness. Studies show that after TM, reactions are faster, creativity greater, and comprehension broader.

A laboratory study of practitioners of Maharishi Mahesh Yogi's transcendental meditation (TM), carried out by Benson and Wallace at Harvard Medical School towards the end of the 1960s, provided the first detailed knowledge of the many physiological changes that go with meditation.

Some of the meditators, whose ages ranged from seventeen to forty-one, had been meditating only a few weeks, others for several years. All recorded changes associated with deep relaxation.

The fall in metabolic rate was the most striking discovery. This was indicated by a dramatic drop in oxygen consumption within a few minutes of starting meditation. Consumption fell by up to twenty per cent below the normal level; below that experienced even in deep sleep. Meditators took on average two breaths less and one litre less air per minute. The meditators' heart rate was several beats less per minute.

During meditation, blood pressure stayed at 'low levels', but fell markedly in persons starting meditation with abnormally high levels.

The meditators' skin resistance to an electrical current was measured. A fall in skin resistance is characteristic of anxiety and tension states; a rise indicates increased muscle relaxation. The finding was that though meditation is primarily a mental technique, it soon brings significantly improved muscle relaxation.

Meditation reduces activity in the nervous system. The parasympathetic branch of the autonomic or involuntary nervous system predominates. This is the branch responsible for calming us.

During anxiety and tension states there is a rise in the level of lactate in the blood. Lactate is a substance produced by metabolism in the skeletal muscles. During meditation blood lactate levels decreased at a rate four times faster than the rate of decrease in non-meditators resting lying on their backs or in the meditators themselves in pre-meditation resting.

The likely reason for the dramatic reduction in lactate production by meditators was indicated when further studies of meditators showed an increased blood flow during. Benson and Wallace found that there was a thirty-two per cent increase in forearm blood flow. Lactate production in the body is mainly in skeletal muscle tissue; during meditation the faster circulation brings a faster delivery of oxygen to the muscles and less lactate is produced.

The two investigators summed up the state produced by their meditating subjects as wakeful and hypometabolic. The physiological changes were different in many ways from those found in sleeping people or those in hypnotic trance states. Meditation, they said, produces 'a complex of responses that marks a highly relaxed state'. Moreover, the pattern of changes they observed in meditators suggested an integrated response, mediated by the central nervous system.

"Through meditation we can learn to access the relaxation response (the physiological response elicited by meditation) and to be aware of the mind and the way our attitudes produce stress," says Dr Borysenko, author of *"Minding the Body, Mending the Mind"*. "In addition, by quieting the mind, meditation can also put one in touch with the inner physician, allowing the body's own inner wisdom to be heard."

Taoists believe that the mind of emotions is governed by the Fire energy of the heart. When your emotions are not controlled, the fire energy of the heart flares upwards, wastefully burning up energy and clouding the mind. The mind of intent, or willpower, is controlled by the Water energy of the kidneys. When unattended, the water energy flows down and out through the sexual organs, depleting essence and energy and weakening the spirit. Taoists believe that when you are 'sitting still, doing nothing', as in meditation, the flow of Fire and Water are reversed: Water energy from the kidneys and sacrum is drawn up to the head via the Central and Governing channels, while emotional Fire energy from the heart is drawn down into the Lower Elixir Field in the abdomen, where it is refined and transformed and enters general circulation through the energy channels. On the spiritual/mental level, this internal energy alchemy enables the mind of intent (Water) to exert a calming, cooling, controlling influence over the mind of emotion (Fire).

Prayer (Ref 1)

In August 1998, Duke University reported that a study of 4000 North Carolinians ages 65 or over found those who participated in religious activities were 40 per cent less likely to have high blood pressure which increases risk of heart disease. Research has shown that religious people are less depressed, have healthier immune systems and deal better with addictions than the non-religious.

Prayer has been used as a healing tool for centuries. And now, the scientists have proof that it really does work.

New York Jets defensive end Dennis Byrd is paralyzed after breaking his neck during a football game, and doctors tell him he will never walk again — yet today he does.

A clinical psychologist in California is diagnosed with non-Hodgkin's lymphoma; the cancer spreads even after surgery, but months later a CAT scan shows no evidence of disease.

A 10-month-old boy is dying of pneumonia after undergoing a liver transplant; doctors give him just two days to live — yet within 24 hours, his fever is gone and he is on the path toward full recovery.

The football player, the psychologist, and the child have something in common that explains their recovery against all odds. In each case, while medical care certainly played a role, ultimately it was prayer that brought their remarkable recovery.

Invoking divine intervention has been a standard approach to healing across cultures for thousands of years. Medical researchers, reluctant until recently to acknowledge a link between faith and recovery, are now concluding that, indeed, praying may make sick people better. A team at the National Institutes of Health (NIH) reviewed more than 250 studies published since the nineteenth century and found a positive connection between prayer and healing for nearly every kind of cancer, cardiovascular disease, hypertension, colitis, and enteritis.

There is even evidence that patients who are prayed for by friends, family, or prayer groups — sometimes hundreds of miles away — are more likely to recover faster from illnesses than those who have nobody praying on their behalf.

"We're beginning to see that having faith in God, a higher power that listens, cares, and responds, can be a very powerful force in healing," says Harold G. Koenig, M.D., director of the Programme on Religion, Aging, and Health at Duke University Medical Center in Durham, N.C. "All the evidence says that prayer does have an impact."

Kenneth Pargament, Ph.D., a psychologist and researcher at Bowling Green State University in Bowling Green, Ohio said, "We can't measure God directly, but we can measure the impact of belief. We can look at the footprints in the sand, the footprints left by faith."

Spiritual Healing

Spirituality involves the recognition and acceptance of a God beyond our own intelligence and with whom we can have a relationship. This God can provide an experience of inspiration, joy, security, peace of mind, and guidance that goes beyond what is possible in the absence of the conviction that such a power exists.

Spiritual healing is when energy is transmitted to the person who needs it. The treatment works on the body, mind and spirit, which are seen as one unit that must harmonize for good health. If a separate healer is involved, the healer will place the hand on the person being treated to channel the energy from the Higher Source. The spiritual healing can help mental and emotional problems and physical conditions such as a frozen shoulder.

What is Spiritual Healing?

The channeling of healing energy from its spiritual source to someone who needs it is called spiritual healing. The channel is usually a person, whom we call a healer, and the healing energy is usually transferred to the patient through the healer's hands. The healing does not come from the healer, but through him. On the other hand, you don't need a healer to take advantage of spiritual healing. You can pray.

The word "spiritual" refers to the divine nature of the energy, which healers agree comes from one external, invisible intelligent source. The healing energy from this source is available to all.

Healers see the body mind and spirit as one interdependent unit and believe all three must work in harmony to maintain positive health. Any problem, be it a broken leg or depression needs the power of healing to restore the balance of the whole person. It is felt that sickness often starts in the mind, or at the deeper level of the spirit, and it is often here that healing begins.

New Age and the Dawning of a New Era

New Age is a loose term that includes everything from self-improvement programmes to awareness of mind-body connections. The movement is growing by leaps and bounds.

Time magazine reported that in 1996, about 44 million Americans identified with the healing movement. It is estimated that Americans alone spend about $1.5 billion annually on books about spirituality and religion. About 42 per cent of Americans have sought out alternative health care. So, there is no doubt that the movement is catching on.

"There is a hunger for being connected with a divine force. The hunger is not just for philosophy, but for experience," says James Redfield, author of *'Celestial Prophecy'*.

"The consciousness I am describing – the perception of synchronisticity, mysterious coincidences – represent great opportunities to grow. That process works whether you are a brain surgeon or sacking groceries. Consciousness has the ability to break cycles of poverty."

Spirituality vs. Religion (Ref 1)

Spirituality can be seen as being distinct from religion. Different world religions have proposed various doctrines and belief systems about the nature of a God and humanity's relationship with it. Spirituality, on the other hand, refers to the common experience behind these various points of view. It is an experience involving an awareness of and relationship with something that transcends your personal self as well as the human order of things. This "something" has been given various names ("God" being the most popular in Western Society) and defined in ways that are too numerous to count. We call it simply as the God. You can choose to define what that means for yourself in whatever way feels most appropriate. Your own sense of a God can be as abstract as "cosmic consciousness" or as down-to-earth as the beauty of the ocean or mountains. Even if you regard yourself an agnostic or atheist, you may get a sense of inspiration from taking a walk in the forest or contemplating a beautiful sunset. Or a small child's smile may give you a special sense of joy.

Dr Herbert Benson of Harvard University and author of *'Relaxation Response'* conducted scientific experiments to determine efficacy of prayer or mantra. Benson believed that there is no magic to the mantra. He taught people to meditate using the word one or any other phrase they felt comfortable. He studied Christians and

Jews who pray regularly. He asked Catholics to use their mantra phrases such as, "Hail Mary, full of grace" or use the Jesus Prayer. Jews used the peace greeting, "Shalom" or "Echad," meaning one. Protestants used the first line of the Lord's Prayer, "Our father, who art in heaven," or "Lord is my shepherd," the opening of the twenty-third psalm. Initially, all these mantras worked equally well in invoking the relaxation response and stimulating the healthful physiological changes in the body as a result of it. But Benson also found that those who used the word one or similar simple phrases that had no particular spiritual meaning did not stick with the programme whereas those who used prayers continued because of their belief. It has also been scientifically shown that to be effective, the person using the prayer of mantra has to have an unqualified faith that it will work. This is described by the scientists as intrinsic belief, characterised by profound spiritual commitment, devotion and quest for a truly transformed life. Thus, religious component in the spirituality is certainly very useful, and in fact may be needed, before the full benefits of spiritual healing can be realised.

There is much healing and benefit to be obtained by cultivating your spiritual life. A personal spiritual commitment is the most important ingredient. Spiritual awareness and growth can effect a transformation in your whole being. It can help you to develop a basic trust and faith that is unshakable. Scientists call this intrinsic belief.

Many have experienced major turnarounds in their condition as a result of cultivating their spirituality. They feel that developing a relationship with their God provided the moral support, courage, hope, and faith for them to follow through with their personal recovery programme. It provided them with a sense that they are not alone in the universe, and that there is a source of guidance and support that is available at times of confusion and discouragement.

Specific Benefits of Developing Your Spirituality

Edmund Bourne, author of *'The Anxiety and Phobia Workbook,'* has described a number of benefits to spirituality as it applies to healing emotional problems. Dr Burke has personal experience of his patients benefiting from a deep spirituality. He has listed a number of benefits that are gained through spirituality. These are:

Security and Safety

Through developing a connection with God, you gain security through the conviction that you are not all alone in the universe, even at those times when you feel temporarily separated from other people. You feel increasingly safe as you come to believe that there is a source you can always turn to in times of difficulty. As the twenty third psalm says, "God is my shepherd," he will take care of me and won't let me get into trouble if I trust him. There is much security to be gained through the understanding that there is no problem or difficulty that cannot be resolved through the help of God.

Peace of Mind

Peace of mind is the result of feeling a deep, abiding sense of security and safety. The more reliance and trust you develop in God, the easier it becomes to deal without fear or worry with the inevitable challenges life brings. It is not that you give up your self or your will to such a power; rather you simply learn that you can "let go" and turn to God when you feel stuck with a problem in living and don't know how to proceed. Learning how to let go when solutions to problems aren't immediately apparent can go a long way toward reducing worry and anxiety in your life. Peace of mind is what develops in the absence of such anxiety.

Self-Confidence

As you develop a relationship with God, you come to realise that he has created you and hence he has found something good in you. You are part of the universe. You're good, lovable, and worthy of respect just by virtue of the fact that you're God's creation. This realisation can improve the way you look at yourself and will help you to improve your ego and what you think of yourself. You are still inherently good and worthwhile. Your own judgments of yourself, however negative, do not ultimately count if you are a creation of the universe as much as everything else. As one person put it: "God doesn't make junk."

The Capacity to Give and Receive Unconditional Love

The most fundamental characteristic of God is that it offers you an experience of unconditional love. This is a kind of love which differs from romantic love or even ordinary friendship. It entails an absolute caring for the welfare of another without any preconditions. That is, no matter how another person appears or acts, you have compassion and care for them without judgment. As you develop a deeper connection with God, you come to experience greater degrees of unconditional love in your life. You feel your heart opening more easily to people and their concerns. You feel freer of judgment toward them or of making comparisons among them. Unconditional love shows up both in your increased capacity to give love to others and to experience more of it coming into your life. You begin to experience less fear and more joy in your life and help to inspire others to experience their own capacity for unconditional love. This kind of love also manifests itself through the experience of having everything you need in your life to get on with what you want to do.

Guidance

Developing a relationship with God will provide you with guidance for making decisions and solving problems. God has a universal wisdom that goes beyond what you can accomplish through your own intellect. In traditional religions this has been referred to as the "divine intelligence". Through connecting with God, you can draw upon this greater wisdom to help you resolve all kinds of difficulties. By learning to ask God for guidance, you'll be surprised to find that every sincere request sooner or later is answered. And the quality of that answer generally exceeds what you could have figured out through your own conscious intellect or will. Here, God is like your co-pilot. God is always available in the instant of need to those who have made a habit of waiting quietly before Him for insight and guidance.

Follow these guidelines for an effective relationship with God:

- Be quiet, patient, and open before God.
- Be confident that he will communicate his wishes and help you execute them.

- Do not tempt God or make terms with Him. Gandhi said, "Not until we have reduced ourselves to nothingness, can we conquer the evil in us. God demands nothing less than complete self-surrender as the price for the only real freedom that is worth having. And when a man thus loses himself, he immediately finds himself in the service of all that lives. It becomes his delight and his recreation."
- Be willing to accept what God provides. He knows best. "Thy will, not mine, be done." Have full trust in the wisdom of God.
- Ask for God's help. Do not instruct him on what to do.
- Let God speak to you through his Word. Read spiritual and religious books such as the Bible and learn about the rules of victorious living.

These are some of the characteristics that define a close relationship with God. All of them can significantly contribute to your personal healing process. The extent and sincerity of your commitment will determine the degree of personal healing you experience.

Outside Help: Healing Practitioners, Intercessory Prayers, etc.

Healers

Healers believe that everyone has a healing mechanism that flows as an energy force around the body, mind and spirit to keep them in perfect order. Unfortunately, stress, an inadequate diet, a negative attitude and other adverse factors can block our healing mechanism so that it cannot function correctly and we get ill. Spiritual healing provides the energy needed to crank our own healing mechanism back into action. When a healer lays his hand on you, he acts as a conductor or channel for the healing energy which he believes has the "intelligence" to go where it is needed.

Healers say that all of us have the power to heal, if we choose to develop it. However, some do seem to have a healing gift.

Healing does not always work at a physical level; the illness may remain but the ability to cope with it improves. Sometimes it does not work at all. This may be because the sick person "blocks" the healing forces - some people subconsciously prefer to be ill. It may also be because we "need" to remain ill.

Healing is not just about living well, but also dying well. People healed when they are dying may die more peacefully.

Typically, to begin the treatment the healer will attune with the healing energy. Then he may scan your body, with his hands hovering just above you. This scanning is to take a reading of your body's energy levels and to locate areas of low or blocked energy where healing is needed. How long the healer spends on each area is determined by your body's needs. Generally, the session lasts about an hour. All healers work in this way, but some employ additional healing tools such as visualisation, past lives therapy, aura healing or they may concentrate on using the "chakras" the seven main energy centres of the body.

During the treatment you may feel heat coming from the healer's hands, although some people feel a draught, a tingling sensation, pins and needles, or a feeling of fight-headedness. Afterwards, most people say they feel relaxed and peaceful, although you might feel thirsty or sleepy. Leave a few days or a week between sessions to give the healing time to work.

Intercessory Prayers

Many Christians ask saints and others to intercede on their behalf. People pray for others. Your chance of healing can be improved substantially if you can get others to pray for you. The scientific evidence for the efficacy of such prayers is described elsewhere.

Which Problems Can Spiritual Healing Help?

Spiritual healing can help with any problem, mental, physical or emotional. Healers are especially effective for musculo-skeletal problems, such as frozen shoulders, stiff necks and bad knees.

What Can You Do to Develop Your Spiritual Life

You can deepen your commitment to spirituality through any of the following means:

- Regular participation in church or temple or your preferred spiritually based organisation.

- Regular reading of inspirational literature of your preference. It's good to do this at least once per day, either upon awakening, during your lunch break, or before retiring.
- Regular practice of meditation.
- Regular practice of prayers.
- Get help from others (Healing practitioners, intercessory prayer, etc.).
- Join a prayer group or get involved in a 12-step programme that is relevant to your needs. (The 12-step programmes offer many people a well-conceived and effective approach for healing addictions. Although they began with Alcoholics Anonymous 50 years ago, they now include a wide range of programmes such as Emotions Anonymous, Co-Dependents Anonymous, and so on.

Chapter - 10

An Integrated Approach to Stress Management

> "Meditation is both the symbol and expression of our intention to grow. Sitting still, alone with our thoughts and feelings, we can honour missed opportunities, passing desires, remembered disappointments, as well as our inner strength, personal wisdom, and ability to forgive and love."
>
> —*Sebastian Pole*

In the previous Chapters of this book, we have discussed elaborately and shared with you, knowledge on details pertaining to stress management, which have already been researched upon and is available in various formats by various experts and authors, for the reader to see read and assimilate. To recapitulate, we have, in total, shared a lot of knowledge on the following topics of interest on stress management (Ref 1, 3, 4, 5, 8, 9, 10, 11, 12).

- Definition, Nature and Mechanism of Stress
- Classification, Sources, Personality Types and Stress
- Symptoms of Stress – Warning Signs
- The Effects of Stress on Systems in the Body
- Coping With Stress: Remedial Actions
- Changing our thinking
- Changing our behaviour
- Changing our life style
- Spirituality – The Ultimate concepts related to managing stress

Under coping with stresses, we have dealt with several techniques under each of the following headings. Let us briefly recollect some of them.

Changing Our Thinking

- Reframing
- Positive thinking

Changing Our Behaviour

- Assertiveness
- Get Organised/Time Management
- Ventilation
- Humour
- Laughter
- Playing with children and learning from them
- Diversion and Distraction

Changing Life Style

- Diet
- Exercises
- Relaxation
- Drink Water
- Deep Breathing
- Nature Walks and Imagery
- Hydrotherapy: A Warm, Hot Bath
- Music Therapy
- Sleep

Spirituality as Part of Life Style Changes

- Yoga
- Meditation
- Prayer
- Spiritual healing

Stress Management is a vast subject. There may be several more techniques meant for taking away stress from one's life. The methods depend upon the person and the personality. What appears as stress to one person may be a way to have relaxation and fun to another person depending on the nature, attitude, likings and dislikings of the individual.

In the above discussions, we have not expanded in any great detail, hobbies and games like Tennis, cricket, hockey, soccer etc. We have also not talked about the use of martial arts as a means of self-defence while they serve as tools of physical fitness, mental strength and means of self-realisation, peace and spirituality. The point is that the scope of the book is immense and can easily move in to all walks of our life.

So, we are not going to delve into the entire range of techniques and tools available for keeping oneself healthy, fit, stress-free, peaceful and happy. It is neither possible nor practical to cover all those topics in one book.

We come then to the primary objective of this book. The aim of this book is to enable the reader to learn that stress is part of life and one should know that it exists in various forms, physical, mental and emotional. It needs to be accepted, faced and combated at times. One needs to acquire knowledge for that purpose. Above all, one needs to apply this knowledge in our daily lives to overcome the negative effects of stress and stay positive. Spirituality and associated techniques aid and enhance this process of living.

In addition to what has been said above, we now wish to emphasise a key point which is important among the primary objectives of this book, not to be missed. That is to tell the reader that there are no specific miracle tools for a specific kind of stress related disorders. Instead, one has to use all the techniques one has learned in an INTEGRATED MANNER depending on stressful issues one faces in different circumstances, on a daily basis, stay happy, healthy and peaceful. That is a very important purpose of this book. We are going to talk about this integrated approach to stress management in the following paragraphs of this book in a slightly more elaborate way with more clarity.

An Integrated Approach to Stress Management

What is an integrated approach to stress management? We have read in the foregoing chapters, obtained knowledge and become aware of the various means of coping with stress which we have summarised in the previous sections of this concluding chapter. These include:

(a) Methods of changing patterns of thinking such as reframing, positive thinking.

(b) Methods of changing patterns of behaviour such as learning to be more assertive, managing time in an effective and organised manner, practicing humour, laughter, ventilation, playing with and learning from children, practicing diversion and distraction techniques.

(c) Methods of changing patterns of life style habits such as diet, exercises, relaxation, drinking water, deep breathing, nature walks and imagery, hydro-therapy, warm water bath, music therapy, correcting sleep patterns.

(d) As part of life style changes, gaining knowledge and practicing spirituality initiatives such as yoga, various kinds including hatha yoga, meditation on a daily basis, faith and prayer, all of which can lead to spiritual healing of the physical and mental ailments, disorders and diseases.

Integrated approach to stress management would mean given a specific individual, specific stress issues in specific circumstances, checking all the above techniques and more, one by one, to the existing stress issues in context, selecting those that will be of help immediately and in the long-term and applying them to rake in benefits in a systematic and organised way. This would mean elimination of all the anxiety and panic reactions of any kind in tackling issues. It would mean a peaceful manner in which any type of stress would be managed by the individuals needing solutions. It would invariably mean total mastery and control in handling difficult circumstances of any kind.

The best way, the author thinks, to make the reader understand the core of this message is through a case study. Since he has been a teacher in higher level education in management for over two decades, he believes in the methodology of case studies even in this modern era of e-learning through the internet. This is not to undermine the value of technology as a learning tool. Let us proceed to look at the case in question.

Case of Vaibhav, the Retired old Professional

Vaibhav has retired two years ago from a corporate job of responsibility and authority. He is sixty two. He has a problem. He is not only retired, but is bored in life too. He is bugged by several problems, none of which are financial. However, most of his problems are physical and mental in nature.

For example, Vaibhav is very obese, since he never did exercises his long innings with corporates. He was hard working, though, sacrificing several personal hours with his wife and children, for work in the office. He has developed illnesses like diabetes and high blood pressure due to his past life style. Recently, a check-up with the doctor revealed that the health problems do not seem to abate, instead, seem to be on the increase.

Vaibhav continues to eat and drink without control, does no exercise despite the doctor's warnings and does not heed to advice. Recently, he has become a victim of psychological problems like depression. He feels life is useless after retirement. He has withdrawn to himself and does not talk to even members of his family. He is tired and exhausted. He is, of late, thinking of even ending his life. His family members, especially his wife is very apprehensive. Vaibhav's negativity is beginning to affect her too in a big way. She consulted a spiritual guru of hers. Vaibhav has no belief in God and refuses to meet the Guru for guidance.

Some of the hobbies Vaibhav is passionate about, despite his many negative ones, happen to be reading books and watching TV.

What do you think should be done, in order that Vaibhav becomes normal, happy, healthy, and peaceful and his life begins to move smoothly, along with the lives of the members of his family?

The Solution to the Case of Vaibhav - An Integrated Approach to His Stress

Vaibhav is a typical case of a person who has neglected and continues to neglect his health like, any people we encounter in our daily lives. He is also one, who does not listen to people because he is too egoistic. The author would like to analyse his case and apply the knowledge he has shared with the reader in a systematic way in order to suggest a solution to the challenge of bringing Vaibhav back to health and happiness. Here are the author's thoughts and suggestions.

Vaibhav does not like advice from people easily. However, fortunately, he enjoys watching TV and reading books. Vaibhav can be encouraged to read a book on 'Stress Management' like the one the author has published. May be his wife can buy this book and present it to him for him to read on his own, without pressing him much. He will do the reading himself.

He can be encouraged by his wife to watch sports channels on TV of his choice. This will enable him to watch sports men, fitness experts, body builders and so on. The desire to be fit physically and mentally has to come from within Vaibhav. This will emerge out of freewill and not compulsion.

Changing the Thinking Patterns

Vaibhav must be encouraged to think positively. Since he is unfit and depressed as a retired man, he should be made to reframe his thinking in to understanding that retirement is an opportunity to relax and do slowly all the things that he had desired to do.

Vaibhav requires psychological counselling in this area and must be introduced to people who are still active in old age, people who do social work, people with disabilities, which manage themselves very well and are contributive to society also and not a burden.

Changing the Behaviour Patterns

Vaibhav can change his behaviour pattern in the following areas.

In retirement, with more time in hand, he can do time management in a different way, allocating more time in daily routines for activities like walking, exercises, reading, listening to TV, music etc. He can also do some part-time work as an adviser or consultant to some organisations needing his skill.

He can develop new friends in the community in which he lives. He can develop friendship with older, retired guys who are still active, doing useful work. He can try and associate with people doing work for NGOs involved in social causes like helping under privileged children, visually challenged children, old people needing help etc.

He should have at least one close friend in whom he can confide and share his problems and ventilate thoughts.

He should practice laughter and humour in greater measures in order to remain relaxed and easy under all circumstances.

Playing with small children in his own house like grand children or in the neighbourhood helps him to think young, gain and learn from the innocence and positive energy of children will help him manage his negative attitudes and stresses in a much better way.

Whenever Vaibhav feels overwhelmed by thoughts which are very negative, he should try and distract himself from such thoughts by doing activities which he has enjoyed doing like listening to music or watching a nice sports event on TV so that the thoughts get diverted and he can regain balance in a short span of time.

We will discuss techniques like meditation and prayer under the banner spirituality in daily life.

Changing Life Style Patterns

The first thing Vaibhav has to accomplish so far as life style patterns are concerned is diet. Apparently, since he is an obese individual who has not been used to exercises in his life before retirement, he has to look at his eating habits to reduce excess fat and weight in order to trim down. He has to, with the help of a doctor or a dietrician, eat a balanced food high in nutrition, less in fat, adequate in protien, vitamins and minerals. He need to drink enough water, eat enough fiber in the form of salads and so on. He needs to keep checking his weight often and bring his weight under control without resorting to obsessions like excessive fasting.

On the exercise front, Vaibhav has to resort to simple exercises like walking, stretching, gentle cycling to keep knees and legs strong and muscular. Straight away jumping in to strenuous workouts in gym etc., must be avoided. A combination of walking and limited jogging can be resorted to daily, in order to bring the body under control and tone. When the fitness level improves, may be, he can combine workout in a gym, three times a week, under the guidance of an expert. Vaibhav needs not to do any one thing excessively. Experience will teach him to stay fit in the long run. Positive results in this area will motivate him further.

Vaibhav needs to relax more, drink plenty of water, do a lot of deep breathing exercises, especially when confronted by pressures from within and outside. He should go to places containing water like a river or a sea front during week-end and if not possible, once in a month for a change and enjoy the outings which could rejuvenate and nurse him back to good mood, cheer and health.

Vaibhav seems to like music. So, he should listen to music which is close to his heart, be it classical, karnatic, Hindustani, filmi, light music, western classical, whatever be his choice as often as he wishes in a day. He can listen to music which soothes him into a good sleep before he hits the bed at night. Vaibhav can contemplate on the idea of going to music master, even at this age, to learn some form of music in a formal way in order to acquire more skill and proficiency. His will give him more satisfaction, self-esteem, peace and happiness during and at the end of the process.

Sleep

Going to bed early and getting up early in the morning should become a habit for Vaibhav. Before going to bed, he can read good books of value, meditate or say prayers if he believes in God. Entertaining negative thoughts is a habit he should not indulge in. He should drop all the negative things which happened during the day, vow not to repeat mistakes which occurred due to his errors, relax and go to sleep. Listening to nice, soothing music before he closes his eyes will be a good habit he can cultivate in order to have a sound sleep which will refresh his body and mind from exhaustions he might suffer during the day.

Spiritual Practices which Can Benefit Vaibhav

Practising spirituality is indeed is a life style pattern. However, as we have mentioned earlier, it is discussed separately in this case study of an individual suffering stress because it helps the reader understand its significance with more clarity for better use and effectiveness in life.

Yoga Asanas (Hatha Yoga) to make the body supple and relax the mind too, can be learnt by Vaibhav from a teacher. They can be done regularly, a few at one time, along with exercises like walking etc. Three days of exercises and three days of yoga alternately with one full day's rest will be an ideal combination for him.

If Vaibhav is a believer, he should combine yoga and meditation with daily prayers in the morning and at night. He can develop the habit of praying often if he is spiritually more inclined and believes in God more.

Spirituality for self-realisation and enlightenment is a separate pursuit Vaibhav can indulge in, provided he is driven by a desire to do so. Else, he can restrict these practices just for physical and mental stress management. The choice is entirely his. The author does not advise anyone reading this book that without prayer or meditation life will be unfulfilled. However, he wishes to emphasise that combined with all the techniques suggested by him in this book, if the reader develops an attitude to listen and learn more about the use of spiritual pursuits in life, the beneficiary is him and him only.

Conclusion – The Integrated Approach to Stress Management

The case study of Vaibhav is a classical example which illustrates how managing stress in one's life is not straightforward with single point solutions. It is a challenge which requires an integrated approach first based on knowledge regarding the techniques required like positive thinking, changing behavioural patterns and life style patterns which have been a result of many years of repetition of habits from childhood, hard to forget and erase. It would mean a lot of again repetitive efforts in the right direction to undo the negativity of the wrong patterns inculcated and relearning of the right ones. This will, again vary from case to case and there are no fixed solutions. Spirituality goes a long way, the author has indicated, through the case study example to help individuals to overcome stress issues in life, lead a more balanced, peaceful, happy and healthy life.

The author wishes the reader a happy journey during the course of gaining knowledge on stress management and applying the techniques learned in an integrated manner to enjoy more fulfilment, health, happiness, peace and prosperity in life.

God Bless You!

Bibliography

1. Wikipedia, the free encyclopedia, 'Stress Management', Dec 2015.
2. 'Management of Stress', Chapter 11, Organisational Behaviour, Dr. Anjali Ghanekar, ISBN-81-86314-12-1, Everest Publishing House, Pune.
3. 'Stress Management and the Science of Living', Dr. Viswanathan Gopalan, International Conference, VIPSAR, Indore, 2012.
4. 'Stress Management and the science of Living', Dr Viswanathan Gopalan, ISSN Journal, VIPSAR, 2013.
5. Selye, H (1950). "Stress and the general adaptation syndrome". Br. Med. J. 1 (4667): 1383–92.
6. Lazarus, R.S., and Folkman, S. (1984). Stress, Appraisal and Coping. New York: Springer.
7. Somaz, Wenk Heidi and Tulgan, Bruce (2003). Performance Under Pressure: Managing Stress in the Workplace. Canada. HRD Press Inc., pp. 7-8. ISBN 0-87425-741-7.
8. Sedgeman, J.A. (2005). Health Realisation/Innate Health: Can a quiet mind and a positive feeling state be accessible over the lifespan without stress-relief techniques? Med. Sci. Monitor 11(12) HY47-52. [1]
9. Lehrer, Paul M.; David H. (FRW) Barlow, Robert L. Woolfolk, Wesley E. Sime (2007). Principles and Practice of Stress Management, Third Edition. pp. 46–47. ISBN 1-59385-000-X.
10. Bower, J. E. and Segerstrom, S.C. (2004). "Stress management, finding benefit, and immune function: positive mechanisms for intervention effects on physiology". Journal of Psychosomatic Research 56 (1): 9–11. doi:10.1016/S0022-3999(03)00120-X. PMID 14987958.

11. Schultz and Schultz, D (2010). Psychology and work today. New York: Prentice Hall. p. 374.
12. Hardy, Sally (1998). Occupational Stress: Personal and Professional Approaches. United Kingdom: Stanley Thornes Ltd. pp. 18-43.

Index

T

V

W

Y